Too scared to tell till now

Too
scared
to
tell

till

now

Tricia Cook

GRANVILLE ISLAND
PUBLISHING

Publisher's Cataloging-in-Publication Data

Names: Cook, Patricia, author.
Title: Too scared to tell till now : a woman's journey to a fulfilled life / Patricia Cook.
Description: Vancouver, BC: Granville Island Publishing, 2019.
Identifiers: ISBN 978-1-926991-98-6 (pbk.) | 978-1-989467-07-7 (ebook)
Subjects: LCSH Cook, Patricia. | Adult child sexual abuse victims—Biography. | Adult child abuse victims—Biography. | Women—Canada--Biography. | Canada—Emigration and immigration—Biography. | BISAC BIOGRAPHY & AUTOBIOGRAPHY / Personal Memoirs | FAMILY & RELATIONSHIPS / Abuse / Child Abuse
Classification: LCC HV6570.2.C64 2019 | DDC 362.7/64/092—dc23

ISBN 978-1-926991-98-6 (paperback)
ISBN 978-1-989467-07-7 (ebook)

Book editor: Sam Margolis
Cover designer: Paul DuVernet
Book designer: Omar Gallegos
Proofreader: Rebecca Coates

Granville Island Publishing Ltd.
212 – 1656 Duranleau St. Granville Island
Vancouver, BC, Canada V6H 3S4

604-688-0320 / 1-877-688-0320
info@granvilleislandpublishing.com
www.granvilleislandpublishing.com

I would like to dedicate my book first to my loving husband, John, his love, support and encouragement in helping me be myself. To my son and two daughters for the love they have shown me throughout their lives. To our granddaughter, who brought a great deal of sunshine. And to my sister Barbara, for the support and encouragement to get my book finished.

I will love you all always

Contents

Canada: 1967 – 1985

Finding Happiness: 1985 – present

Foreword

Too Scared to Tell till Now is a brutally honest page-turner. It must have been very difficult to write. I finished it with great admiration for Tricia Cook, the author, who faced many serious setbacks in her life but always seemed to find a way to go on to new challenges and to make significant contributions to her community.

This autobiography begins with her childhood growing up in the north of England during World War II in a dysfunctional family with a sexually abusive father and a super strict mother. It continues through her early adulthood as a student nurse, her marriage and the birth of her children, and the young family's move to Canada. Marriage breakdown and subsequent remarriage follow.

Themes are sexual abuse, stressful childhood, young mother-hood, immigration, marriage breakdown, disability issues and the challenges that women face when they decide to leave their marriages and well-defined roles as wives and mothers. The author's poetry describes what was going on in her mind at specific intervals and adds another key dimension to her inspiring story.

— *Elspeth Richmond*

Introduction
The Hidden Truth

How do you begin to talk about abuse, let alone write about it? How do I explain the torment of not knowing what to do, or the stress and heartbreak of living with a secret like that? Why would I even think of revealing what happened?

In my late forties I took a course to become a counsellor. I was surprised to learn several of my fellow students were taking the course for the same reason I was — they had all gone through some sort of abuse. They all wanted to help people in the same situation. We were able to talk about it together, and it was quite a weight off my shoulders to know so many others had gone through something similar.

Viewed by modern eyes, what we experienced at school in 1940s and 1950s Yorkshire would be considered abusive. We learned quickly that if we spoke out of turn in the classroom, out would come the cane. I saw children hit on the knuckles and across the hands with rulers. Some were smacked across the backs of their legs by the teacher's hand till their legs were red and raw.

At home things could get volatile. Most of the time Mum and I got along like sisters, but at times her temper would explode. At my tenth birthday party she gave me a leather handbag with a mirror inside. During the party a heavyset mother accidentally sat on it, and I heard the mirror crack. I said to her, "You've broken the mirror, you fat thing!" Afterwards, Mum was so angry she hurled a hot water bottle at me. Thankfully it missed my head, but I could feel the scalding water down my neck and spine.

In most ways I had a normal post-war childhood, with the same experiences, challenges and dreams as millions of other young girls across Britain. Though sex wasn't discussed at home, one tended to pick up things in school. It finally dawns on you that babies have nothing to do with storks.

As I entered puberty, my father became part of our daily lives again after years in the Navy. Things began to happen that I didn't understand. I didn't know what to think about them, or what I should do. Maybe it was wrong to even think such things. It took me quite a while to be certain that accidental touches in private parts were indeed not accidental.

• • •

Who am I? I am a Canadian citizen who came into this world on May 31, 1937, in Kingston upon Hull, England. I am divorced and remarried. I am the mother of three wonderful children — a son and two daughters. I have no pretensions; I was not born with a silver spoon in my mouth. I live a simple everyday life.

Having said that, I believe everyone is special, that each of us is unique. We handle our own problems and stress in many different ways. The same lessons in life may be there for all of us to learn, but positive or negative influences can affect the outcome differently for each individual.

When faced with problems, I think the majority of us feel that no one else could possibly go through what we have gone through, that we are all alone. Suddenly one day, quite by chance, we discover that a neighbour or someone we work with has experienced or is experiencing the same thing. We are quite amazed. Here we are, all in the same boat, never having discussed these problems in the open before.

To be able to share together somehow seems to make our burden a little lighter. We experience a relief and a comfort we have never felt before. We begin to realize that by keeping our problems so well hidden, like secrets in a dark cupboard, we have in fact become our own worst enemy. We have let all the guilt and worry eat us away bit by bit.

Reaching this point and realizing we are not alone, we can now release our secrets into the light. By saying "This has happened to me," we are aware that, yes, it happened — in the past. We have lived through it, and perhaps we can leave it there where it belongs. We are now free to move on with our lives.

Of course, this is very easy to say, but can it really be done? Our backgrounds and the morals we learned early in our lives shape us, and it can take the rest of our lives to change and feel free. Maybe that is why we are given our lives, to learn and accomplish this balance and freedom. Some may do it more quickly than others.

I realized when I reached the age of fifty that I had been searching most of my life to find out who I was. When things kept happening I would ask myself, What am I supposed to be doing here? I had to reflect on most of my life, my childhood in particular, because the good and the bad are all part of who I am today.

It was 1968 when I first put some notes together. Back then, things changed so very quickly and we moved so often that they got filed away. I made up my mind to start again. I would write a few notes and make up some poetry. This time I wasn't going to write just about travels, but about very personal things. I invite you to share some of my stories, in the hope that my experiences will show you that no matter what, so far I have survived, and others can too.

About an ordinary mum

I'm an ordinary mum, just like the rest
Always wanting to do my very best.
I have never been perfect,
but come what may,
I'll keep on trying, day by day.

Yorkshire
1937 – 1953

Early Childhood

On the very last morning of May, into my grandma's house at exactly nine o'clock came a little bundle weighing nine pounds. It had big blue eyes and a shock of bright red hair and would bear the name Patricia. Here I was.

In the spring of 1937, Kingston upon Hull was a hustling, bustling city. The largest fishing port in the world, it was famous for its fleet, which plied the bleak Arctic waters. My family was working class. We lived around the docks on Havelock Street, a long artery of old houses and gas lamps. The street had a fruit store, a grocery store and a bakery. Along the way was a smoked-fish factory, where many Scottish lassies worked. In their break time, they would stand outside in their long rubber aprons with their hands stained dark yellow from the smoked fish, laughing and swearing in their strange Scottish twang.

A sawmill stood at the bottom of the street. As kids we would go there to collect firewood or make footprints in the sawdust. Next door was the city's largest brewery, where large carts laden with huge barrels came and went constantly, pulled by the most splendid shire horses – giant, beautiful piebalds with coats of rich brown and black. Their heads were adorned with brightly coloured plumes and ribbons, and their manes shone like silk.

As well as busy, the street was noisy, especially early in the mornings. You could hear the clatter of clogs on the pavement, worn by the bobbers who worked on the docks and in the fish houses. When the trawlers arrived at the dockside, they swung the baskets of fish, tipping them into metal bins. Then the fish were passed to the bobbers, who chopped off their heads and gutted them, after which they were transferred quickly to the fish markets. It was a very smelly business, but they all wore strong denim dungarees up to their shoulders. As soon as they came home, they changed clothes to get rid of the smell.

We were always proud of our markets and fishmonger shops. The large marble slabs held many varieties of fish and seafood: cockles and mussels, oysters, large crabs and lobsters. Our family treat was to sit around the fireplace with a large bag of winkles. It was quite an art to get the yummy little fish out of the shell all in one piece. We had a straight pin to flick off the tiny scab inside the shell. Years later, it dawned on me that winkles were part of the snail family. I never ate them again.

In addition to fish, there were fresh rabbits and hare. The rabbits lay on the slab, while the hares hung upside down with a cup over their mouths to catch the blood. To this day I have never understood why the hares and not the rabbits were hung upside down. On looking back, I realize there were many things I would never be able to understand.

• • •

My parents were married three years before I was born. They had a small cottage on the edge of the city. Mum was a nurse and Dad was in the Navy, away most of the time. Well into her pregnancy, and with the threat of war, my mum decided to move in with my grandma.

Grandma had been a widow for many years, living on very a small pension with her daughter and son. My cousin Iris, four years older than me, also lived there. Gran had looked after Iris since she was two and a half, though Iris visited her parents regularly. Her mother was delivering her fourth child and her father was away in the Army. Being an only child, I was lucky to have a ready-made sister in Iris. We became very close and to this day I adore her.

Though my dad was at home when I was born, he had to go back to sea three days later. It would be three years before I saw him again. There was always a photo of him on the bedroom mantelpiece to remind me that this man in the sailor clothes was my daddy, who loved us all. Before he left I was given the name Patricia, but through most of my childhood I was called Patsy, a name I came to dislike over the years. It was popular at the time to copy the Royal Family and have three or four names, but Mum would have none of it. She herself had three: Lilian Frances Gertrude. Gran was called Lilian, shortened to Lil, so Mum went by Frances.

I remember that I was extremely shy and very self-conscious in groups. Still, I must have been very naughty at times, because it seemed I was always being punished. Though generous, my mum had a tendency to want to control and dominate everyone. I was punished if I did anything wrong and threatened even when I didn't. I was told I had a very bad temper "as all redheads do."

Our elders were of the Victorian era, very strict. Children, it was believed, should be seen and not heard. It was extremely bad manners to interrupt a grown-up's conversation. If we did, we ran the risk of getting our ears clipped or boxed, or even a belt across the head. We were conditioned to be on our best behaviour at all times and to obey without question.

At times Mum threatened to run away because I had been so bad. When I was in a paddy (temper), I would lie on the floor and go blue in the face. My mum would hold my head under the cold water tap at full force, then lock me in the cupboard for quite a while. I would hear her go down the hallway and bang through the front door. Sitting on the old suitcases, with the odd daddy long legs running across, I would sob in the dark. I recall thinking I had no daddy and now I had lost my mummy. The cupboard was my earliest memory. (During the war, Mum, Gran and I would hide in this cupboard when we couldn't make it down to the bomb shelter in time.) But I realized my mummy always came back.

My second-oldest memory is of my father returning home when I was three. He took us to Glasgow, where we rowed across the loch in a small rowboat I called a *coggy boat*. At night we slept in a regal four-poster bed with curtains all around, something I had never seen before. We were not there long, and soon my dad sailed away again. The next time I saw him was a week after my seventh birthday. In the twenty-two years Dad was in the Navy, he spent fifteen of them abroad.

Our Grandma

Grandma was always the backbone of our family and our street. She ran the household with a firm but loving hand. In our street, she was at everyone's beck and call. If a neighbour was having a baby, they would call her even before the midwife. She was often the one to deliver the baby, or if not, the one to look after the mother for a couple of weeks after the event. She was the same with the sick and dying. The whole street knew her.

Gran had had a hard life. She was the eldest of three children. When she was quite young their father went to work on the docks and disappeared forever. It was presumed he had fallen into the water and been swept out of the River Humber into the North Sea. Years later her mum remarried and had three more children. In those days the schools charged four pence for each child, expensive for a large family. As the eldest, Gran was expected to stay home to help with the children. Her reading and writing were good, but she always regretted that she had fallen short of a full education.

She encouraged us to do well in school and insisted we should never marry early. Though we were told she had married at eighteen, after she died we discovered she had only been sixteen. Gran married a young man from Norfolk who was lodging near her. He came from a well-to-do family but ran away from home to go to sea. They had eight children, six boys and two girls. The children all weighed between ten and thirteen pounds at birth, after which Gran thought that any baby born under nine pounds was a little runt. However, tragedy struck — two of the boys became ill and died within a week of each other. One boy was eighteen months and the other was three and a half years old.

Granddad died when Mum was seventeen and Aunt Ivy, the youngest, was fourteen. The four surviving boys were a few years older and working. Grandma's pension was very small, so to earn extra money she spent her evenings working at home as a net braider, weaving the nets for the fishing trawlers. The nets were made of twine and had to be very neatly woven, and they were so big they had to be hung on a large rod across the door frame. Gran did this for years. In her spare time she taught us how to cut old material into tiny strips, which we hooked to make rugs for the hearth.

Once a week a man would call for the rent and Gran would usher him into the front room, or front parlour as she called it, where the rent money was always kept in the sideboard. If a relative died, this was where the coffin was placed so everyone could pay their respects, and after the funeral we would come back for tea and sandwiches.

Christmas was the only day of the year we could sit in the middle room or dared touch the piano. During the war, our uncles were away at Christmas, but we had so many aunts and cousins, I lost count. Aunt Ivy would play the piano by ear, almost any kind of music, and we'd all sit around singing. We sang "The White Cliffs of Dover" and "Danny Boy," Mum's favourites. She always cried at the end. Despite rationing, our holiday meals were lovely, and they were followed by Christmas pudding and custard. We all got very excited when Gran put silver sixpences and threepenny bits inside for us to find.

Gran had a favourite saying: "No matter how poor you are, there is soap and water." Every time our cousins came over, she inspected their ears. The house was so clean we could have eaten off the floors. A weekly ritual, war or no war, was to clean the brasses from the front and middle room every Saturday. They usually hadn't any finger marks on them to begin with, but if by chance one mark was left on anything, we had to begin again. The only time I ever remember seeing any dust on anything was when our house was bombed.

Our kitchen had a large pantry, and I would sometimes hide in there when no one was about. I would often dip my finger into a new bowl of sugar. Somehow Grandma always knew someone had touched it, and she would run her hand down the front of my dress to feel the telltale grains. Later I learned that whenever she filled the sugar bowl, the sugar poured to a point like a pyramid, and when I poked my finger in, it left a hole in the top.

The washing was done outside in a dolly tub. We twirled around a dolly (a stick with feet) to release the dirt and then rinsed everything under the cold-water tap outside, in both summer and winter. In the summer we hung the washing down the garden on a long line, and in the winter we had a line on the ceiling or a wooden clotheshorse set near the fire.

We had a coalhouse inside the scullery, where sometimes the cat would creep in to find a mouse. One day Aunt Olive, Iris's mother, and I were warming ourselves in front of the fireplace when a tiny mouse ran across the floor. We both yelled together. I made a run to jump up on the chair, but Aunt Olive, a big, tall lady, beat me to it, and in a minute she was on the tabletop. Her head touched the ceiling. I was up on the chair next to her when Grandma entered. "What on earth are you doing up there?" she asked us. We told her a mouse was on the hearth. She said, "You two silly buggers. A little mouse won't hurt you." Gran wasn't scared of anything, and as usual she went after the mouse.

Grandma and Aunty Ivy were very superstitious. Gran had a long list of things that would bring bad luck, such as my habit of swinging the kitchen door with my foot while at the table. The word *pig* couldn't be uttered. Fingernails must not be cut on Friday. If you put any clothes on inside out, like an undershirt or panties, Gran and Aunt Ivy would say "Leave it on, it's unlucky to change it." Never cross two knives. Never throw any bread crusts into the fire. If you see blue flames in the fire, it's the devil coming to get you. If you spill salt, throw a bit over your left shoulder. Through Gran I developed an interest in the supernatural. She said that when she was with the dying, they often talked with people who she later found out were already dead. Her belief was that when we pass away, we never go alone. A relative, friend or angel comes to guide us.

Our grandma was a wonderful, indefatigable lady who made her constant, heavy workload seem easy. People would say to her, "Lil, you'll die with a broom in your hand." Many times she was sick, but she never saw a doctor or a dentist. Her back and fingers were bent with arthritis. She was stone deaf, but she could read lips like reading a book, and always seemed to know what mischief Iris and I got up to.

Her life was devoted to looking after everyone but herself. At age eighty-seven, she was taken into hospital and died within two weeks. She was dearly loved by all. I believe it was everyone's love and respect for her that brought me to care for the elderly later in life. Like Gran, they had so many interesting stories to tell. I found that no matter how difficult that kind of work was, at the end of the day we could always find something to laugh about.

Religion

There were many different churches in Hull — Methodist, Baptist, Wesleyan and Catholic.

I was raised a Protestant and I was never allowed to forget it. Iris and I went to church weekly without fail. Our church, St. Barnabas, was very old but very beautiful. Though we had to go to church every week, the rest of the family only went for weddings, funerals and christenings. After Dad's brother Mac was lost at sea, Mum took us to midnight mass on Christmas Eve. We sang "Eternal Father Strong to Save," and the tears really began to flow when we got to the line "For those in peril on the sea." Midnight mass became a tradition afterwards.

From an early age we were told that people of different skin colours and different faiths weren't like us, and so we didn't mix. There was an Indian man who came around our street often, selling matches to light our fires or candles; we nicknamed him Mr. Matches. His face was so dark brown that I was frightened of him and ran to the other side of the street. My friend Ann kept telling me he was nice and he wouldn't hurt us, but it took me a while to get used to him. The Gypsies who sold us pegs and lucky heather scared me too. They led extraordinary lives, though, travelling from town to town, and their children missed school.

Once when Mum and I were shopping for meat pies for supper, I saw a lovely shop with pies and sausage rolls. Mum said, "We can't go in there."

"Why?" I asked.

"It belongs to Jewish people," she said. "They chop the ends off their little boys' tassels and put them in their pies."

Why did she not tell the truth — that our church disapproved of Jewish people and did not agree with circumcision? I might not have understood it all, but it would have been nice if Mum had tried. But it seemed every question we asked was answered with a made-up story.

Next were Catholics. They got drunk every weekend and then had the audacity to go to church and confess their sins. Very eccentric to us, because even after confession they did it again. The family was irate when Mum's brother John married a Catholic, but I thought they were a very nice couple. Uncle John and Aunt Kathy had three children, Joan, Irene and Michael, who Iris and I got along very well with. A few times when they came to see us, I saw Aunt Kathy lying on the kitchen floor. Mum or Grandma would shout, "Pass me a spoon off the table, then go out to play!" It was strange, almost frightening. Her children never said anything, so I kept wondering why she would want to lie down on the floor. It looked as if they might be putting the spoon in her mouth. As usual I was given no explanation, so I imagined it was just the eccentric behaviour of Catholics.

I must have been about sixteen or seventeen when I heard the true story. Uncle John had once taken Aunt Kathy dancing and she had slipped on the floor and hit her head. Her skull was cracked, so they inserted a silver plate into her head. Soon after, she began to have seizures. Hence the spoon was placed under her tongue to prevent choking.

Later, religious prejudice would have an enormous effect on my marriage. All the grudges about religion caused much heartache for everyone, not to mention the loss of time and the waste of years.

The War Years

I knew in spite of everything that Mum loved me, because she was continually protecting me from a nasty man called Hitler. He was coming after us and we had to fight him together. That was why my daddy had to be away all the time, to protect our country. Her arms held me tight when the bombs were dropping around us. Hull was a major target and suffered a lot of damage. But everyone thought we would get through it as long as we pulled together.

I was nearly three when the Second World War began. Men eighteen and older went off to fight and women had no option but to take up their jobs, a noted shift of the times. In spite of the authoritarian attitude of those born in the Victorian era, a support system unlike any other developed. They sang as they worked to encourage the troops, and they laughed and they cried together. Food became scarce, and everyone had a ration book. A fair system for all — rich and poor alike received the same amount. There was no choice but to share.

Britons were encouraged to grow vegetables, fruit and flowers. Some people bred their own rabbits and chickens for meat and eggs. Rabbits were a problem because they often became pets and thus were hard to kill. I was terrified of the chickens — they were always pecking my legs and ankles. Much later, after they were all gone, their little shed became our favourite playhouse. Its roof was covered with large pink roses, so Iris and I named it Rose Cottage.

We loved our long garden with its three tall lilac trees, one white, one pale purple and the other a very deep purple. Mum would put enormous vases of lilac in the middle room, and the lovely perfume would go all through the house. The garden fences were covered in pink and white roses. There was a patch of mint, a rhubarb bush big enough to hide under, and a gooseberry bush where, I was told, the stork had dropped me off when I was born. It was either the stork or a midwife with a bag. That was the only talk about those sorts of things we heard.

In the garden I used to peep through the fence at our neighbour. We nicknamed him Mr. Robby. He wore baggy pants, a flat cap, an old tweed jacket and a wide black belt of very thick leather around his tummy. Everyone was fascinated by the big white loft he had built on the roof of his air raid shelter. It was full of homing pigeons, which he tended non-stop. They were trained to carry very important messages during the war. Wherever he walked, his little dog followed him. I was shy with most people, but when Mr. Robby spoke to me in his broad Yorkshire accent, he always made me smile.

Nearly everyone had air raid shelters. Ours were large and made of brick, but some had metal shelters designed by Sir John Anderson, a member of the War Cabinet. Inside we had bunks all around the walls to sleep on, and stored blankets and extra food. It was our second home after the bombing.

We could be fined for wasting gas, fuel, food, paper or water. Many pets were put down because they couldn't be fed with anything that might be used for human consumption instead. There was no tinned pet food. Cats lived off mice and odd drops of milk. Soap was rationed and there was no laundry soap or shampoo. We kept our hair short. It became illegal to manufacture makeup. Toothpaste was scarce, so we used salt instead. In lieu of toilet paper, we cut newspapers into squares.

We had electricity in our house but no plugs for vacuums. We took all the rugs outside, hung them on the washing line and beat them with a special tool. With only cold water available, everything had to be boiled. We would wash in our bedrooms, where the dressing tables always had marble tops because we had to pour large jugs of hot water into the basins. We were taught that every part of our body had to be washed daily. Once a week, the giant tin bath was brought in front of the kitchen fire. We were only allowed five inches of water, which we boiled in steel buckets on the stove, and we took turns getting in the bath. It was quite a big job afterwards to scoop out the water and then take the heavy bath out to the backyard and hang it on a nail.

People rarely undressed at night, because there were so many air raids. Many times we didn't make it to the shelter before the bombs started dropping. We hid under the big wooden kitchen table or in the dark cupboard under the stairs. With the bombings and brick dust came lice, fleas and scabies. In those days we rarely heard of allergies – I guess we all got used to the dust, fog and coal fires. The elderly would say, "You'll eat more than a pound of muck before you die."

Iris and I seemed to grow quickly and we had limited stamps to buy clothing. Mum found a dressmaker who made us identical dresses with very deep hems to let down as we got bigger. We were always happy to have hand-me-downs. Shoes had to be strong, laced, and black or brown. I remember Mum sitting on the floor with a cobbler's last (a device to hold shoes) between her legs. To make the shoes last longer, she put studs all around the soles and heels. I was fifteen years old the first time I was able to choose my own shoes. Ever since, I have had a mania for collecting shoes of every colour I can find.

We looked forward to our daily shopping. Before we left, we checked our hands and face and combed our hair. We always carried our own shopping bag. If we forgot to bring one and needed, say, potatoes, the shopkeeper would wrap them in newspaper. Fish and chips were the same, but they had to be wrapped in a sheet of white paper first before being secured in the newspaper. There were many corner shops that sold small quantities to meet our daily needs, and people seemed to enjoy the socializing most of all, chatting with the shopkeepers. With regular news of fatalities, it seemed everyone was under continual stress. I think the external pressure bound us all together.

• • •

I had a friend across the street, Ann, who was five days older than me. We started kindergarten together at a school on Scarborough Street, the next one to ours. The first thing we were given was a new cardboard box to carry everywhere we went — in it was a gas mask in case of chemical warfare. Daily life seemed simple with school so nearby. For breakfast we would sit in front of the fire with a long fork to toast our bread, provided someone, usually Grandma, had made the fire that morning. Later we would come home to lunch. Most days we stopped at the fruit shop to buy a carrot for a halfpenny, or a gammy (bruised) apple for a penny. The unwashed carrot we scraped with a coin.

After school, our chores were to find manure for the garden or wood for the fire. We went to the brewery at the bottom of our street to see if the horses had left anything. If so, we filled our shovels and took it back to the garden. Then it was on to the sawmill, which often left piles of old wood bits outside. Sometimes Gran sent us on an errand to get milk or vinegar. Mr. Hall's shop was a few minutes' walk from our house. We had to take our own jugs and use a ladle to fill them from a metal churn. Milk was easy, but the malt vinegar had to be carried with care. Once I tried to sip it and it splashed in my eye. Boy, did it sting! I never tried again. I kept it only for my fish and chips.

After our errands we played hide and seek with all the children in the street. Sometimes the older children, like Iris, came out and turned the skipping rope we all shared. We also played statues — the first one to move was out of the game. When there were only two of us, we sometimes played a naughty game: knocking on doors and running away. There were quite a few alleys we could hide in. After a few repeated knocks we often heard the people cursing and swearing. We seldom got caught, but if we did we were marched home and got a clip across the ear from our relatives. One thing we learned is that if we did wrong, we would always have to face the consequences.

Dad's brother, Uncle Mac, was on a trawler called the *Commander Horton* that went out to fish one day and totally disappeared. It was believed to have been blown up by a mine, but no remains were found. Sixty years later, my cousin Frank found out on the internet that the Germans had released a list of the ships their submarines had blown up during the war. His dad's ship was on their list. Peace of mind for the family after all those years.

After the *Commander Horton* disappeared, Uncle Mac's two sons, Brian and Frank, were orphans, so they were evacuated to Halifax, a small town in the countryside. Their mum, Aunt Edna, took me, Iris and Mum to visit them at the pretty farm where they were living. It was the first time we had eaten shredded wheat with hot milk. Frank warned us to look out for goats and not to bend over, and we found out what he meant a day or so later. Walking through the cemetery, Frank bent down to fasten his shoelace. Suddenly there was a noise from behind a gravestone. A goat bolted at him and tossed him right over. The goat was on a long chain, but he'd still managed to get Frank.

The air raids continued. Back home, the air wardens came round every night to check our homes for any tiny crack of light. Windows were all covered with black paper blinds, and you could be fined for a sliver of light showing. Even a cigarette outside was light to the enemy. Most of the light bulbs were removed from our rooms so they wouldn't be seen through the skylights, and it was difficult to move from room to room at night. We carried flashlights, but on the long stairs and landings it was scary. Because our toilets were outside, we had to use a chamber pot, or gazunder, as it was known up North, because it "goes under."

One night I was grabbed half-asleep. Everyone was shouting and trying to hurry downstairs. The bombs were all around us. The house was shaking and glass was falling. Then we were walking on glass — all the windows were falling out. We couldn't hide under the table or in the cupboard under the stairs because the door wouldn't open. It took us a while to get out through the garden and into the shelter. Everyone was shaken and upset, thanking God we were still alive.

We were very lucky. When daylight came we saw that half the street on our side was gone, and the other half of the next street as well. In its place was only bricks and rubble, though our school was still standing. At the top of our street was a communal shelter that could hold 500 people. That night there had been 366 people in there. No one had survived. The docks were also damaged, and the death count was high.

We received lots of help from the WVS (Women's Voluntary Service), who came to our aid. This service had been formed in 1938 to assist evacuees. Later they made blankets and knitted socks for our troops, and held classes to teach everyone to darn holes and to patch our clothing. They also formed 1,400 state nurseries so women would be able to take over men's jobs while they fought. We had no gas or electricity, so the WVS brought over mobile kitchens. They provided us with soup, hot meals and dessert — warm custard. It had some wiggly lumps in it, but oh, it was so good!

My mum was sent to work in a munitions factory on the Brough Aerodrome, where they made parts for aircraft. Once, to my excitement, she brought me home a wooden airplane. It was a lovely yellow Spitfire, the airplane chosen to be our national emblem. Aunty Ivy was sent to work as a bus conductor, a big change from her previous job in the metal factory. No matter what kind of job women were given, they seemed to adapt very quickly. It was very strange at times when we looked around for the men — all we seemed to see were elderly ones.

Uncle Ted, a bobber, was called into the Army and sent to Lincolnshire to work on the anti-aircraft searchlights. Iris and I were convinced that when the Germans sent over their planes, he would catch them and keep us safe. A few months later he fell off his bicycle and was crushed by a large army truck. He survived but was an invalid for ten years before dying at fifty-four, a heartache for Grandma, who nursed him till the end.

After the house was damaged in the bombing, we spent most nights snuggling up together in the shelter. We listened to stories and sang war songs. Everyone seemed to enjoy singing. Gracie Fields and Vera Lynn were very popular, and they did so much to entertain our troops. The shelter was damp and smelly, but being together made us feel safe.

The most terrifying thing that could happen, after all the bombing, was to see the telegram boy at your house. We knew he was always the bearer of bad news. Usually it was a big golden envelope from the War Office. A tiny envelope usually meant someone was coming home on leave. Sadly there were more large envelopes than small. You could spot the telegram boy from a distance, riding his bright red motorcycle and wearing a navy blue uniform with red piping down the leg. We always held our breath, wondering who was going to get the bad news.

One day we were almost home from school when Ann said, "The telegram boy is on your doorstep."

"Don't be silly, it must be next door," I said. My heart began to bump as we got nearer and I saw it was indeed my house.

Mum and Grandma were in tears. I had seen Mum cry before, but never Grandma, who was always strong for everyone. I was told my dad's ship, HMS *Enterprise*, had been blown up at sea and he was missing in action. At that time Uncle Ted was still in hospital in critical condition and we didn't know if he was going to live. Now this. I don't think any of us slept for weeks.

We had heard nothing for three weeks, when back came the telegram boy with a gold letter. Everyone held their breath, expecting the worst. Mum almost collapsed when she read the letter. Dad had been found in a hospital in Madagascar, alive but injured. We thanked God and hoped he would be coming home soon. Later Dad told me that when the ship blew up, he and another man had dived for protection. He landed on a table, on top of the other man. The man underneath had had both legs blown off. Dad's legs were hit with shrapnel, and he had the cartilage removed. He was a very lucky man.

Several weeks later, a week after my seventh birthday, I was standing on the railway station with Mum, waiting patiently to meet my dad, now a chief petty officer, for the second time in seven years. The train pulled in, full of troops. I kept looking for the sailors, but there were so many men. I wondered if the train was ever going to empty. A man in uniform stopped at the gate. He looked a bit like our photo, but he had a different kind of hat on. Suddenly Mum smiled and threw her arms around him.

"This is your daddy, Patsy," she said. "Give him a big kiss." I was so stunned, I couldn't. I was too shy. This man was a total stranger to me.

There was a tiny waiting room by the gate, so Mum suggested we go in for a few minutes. Dad gave me the box he was carrying, a special present just for me. I removed the lid to find the most beautiful doll I had ever seen. It was dressed in a pink suede coat and hat, and had bright blue eyes in a familiar face. It was our lovely Princess Elizabeth. I was overwhelmed and finally gave Dad a kiss for such a wonderful present.

It was nice to have Dad home again, but it wasn't long before another telegram arrived telling him to report to a naval base in Chatham. He was going to be there some time, as his new ship was being refitted. He suggested to Mum that we go with him. It would be the first time I had ever been away from Gran and the family. I was excited, and while I would miss Iris and Ann, it was also important to me that I get to know my dad.

On our five-hour train ride to London, we saw troops all over every station we passed. The train was packed tight with servicemen. We had to climb over their kit bags to go to the bathroom or to get a snack. When we got there, London was a very sad sight — miles and miles of bombed buildings, or shells of buildings.

Chatham was further on, and it seemed a very long journey. When we arrived, it felt as though we were in the beautiful, peaceful countryside again. It was an area known for growing hops, and the weather was much warmer than in the North. Dad had rented rooms in a lovely house with a hospitable landlady. The schools were more advanced than the one I had left, but I caught up quickly and made some very nice friends.

Our garden was very overgrown. Our landlady had to work full time, as she had lost her husband and had two teenage boys, who were away. Mum offered to help, since we all loved gardening. There were high-grown weeds and the outside toilet was covered with huge snails, which were up the walls and on the ceiling. I wanted to scream. It was especially scary in the dark, as they crushed under our feet. Mum shovelled them out and scrubbed the outhouse with disinfectant.

One day when we were working in the garden the landlady came through, just setting off for work. Her lovely red hair was dripping with white paint. I wanted to laugh, but Mum said, "Don't you dare. This is nothing to laugh at." We always had said it was unlucky to go under ladders, and that was exactly what she had done. Mum helped her get it off, and in the end she was laughing herself.

Dad seemed ecstatic to have us around. He would bounce me around and tickle my ribs. The landlady's sons had left some boxing gloves behind and Dad, who was a featherweight boxer in the Navy, said he would teach me to box. It was really fun. One day we were boxing without gloves and I tripped over a broom with a split handle and got a huge splinter down my thumbnail. Nobody could get it out, and it began throbbing. We were supposed to go to the pictures and I didn't want to miss it, so we still went. The next morning I was in hospital Emergency under anesthetic. They removed the whole thumbnail. "No more boxing," Mum said. "It's not ladylike." I asked if I could go roller-skating instead. "No, that's for tomboys." I wondered if there would ever be anything I could do of my own choosing.

Chatham was very quiet, though that soon changed when Hitler's V-1 rockets, or doodlebugs, began dropping. They were something new and very scary. My bed was under the window and I could hear the grating noise of the doodlebugs' engines. The noise would stop, a strange quiet would ensue, and then the bomb would drop, causing tremendous damage. Often it seemed so near, I would hide under the blankets. One fell just eight miles away.

After seven months it was time for Dad to go to sea again, and time for us to go home. I had loved my school friends, but I was excited to see my family again. The weekend we returned, the first doodlebug came over Hull. Mum rarely swore, but she said, "Those bloody things have followed us home." We learned later that 8,000 doodlebugs had gone over London and destroyed 25,000 homes.

On June 6, 1944, known as D-Day, the Allied forces invaded France. We thought this was going to end the war, but the bombs kept flying. The bombed-out buildings we played on were slowly being cleared by Italian prisoners of war. We were quite fascinated by them. In their tea breaks they spent time drawing charcoal sketches on anything, and their drawings were very good.

As the war ended, Dad was transferred to HMS *Diadem*, one of the destroyers that would be escorting the Royal Family on their journey to South Africa. It was being refitted in Newcastle upon Tyne, so we travelled to Newcastle to be with Dad for a few months. The school was nice but more advanced, and I hadn't a clue how to do the new division. The worst part was that I was left-handed and they made me use my right hand.

Everywhere we went Mum apologized for my using a spoon in my left hand. It made me nervous and very embarrassed. I always used a knife and fork the correct way — I just couldn't keep a spoon straight in my right hand, automatically swapping it to my left. In those days it was very important to have good table manners.

I began having nightmares, and Mum became worried and took me to the doctor. When he found out I was being made to write with my other hand, he was furious. He said it was clearly affecting my nervous system and it had to stop. He wrote the headmistress, and the nightmares soon ceased.

May 8, 1945, was the end of the war, and people danced and celebrated in the streets. It was time to rebuild and hope for new lives. This part of my life I would never forget. When we go to the cenotaph to celebrate all those who lost their lives, my heart is so full. When the old airplanes do the flyover, it breaks my heart. I hope our stories will be passed on to young people, and I hope the next generations can stop these wars.

My memories from Remembrance Days

I search my mind. What did I see?
What does Remembrance Day mean to me?
The air raid warden starts to shout,
"Put out that light, it's now blackout."
So we'd pull down the blinds and then we sped
Into the air raid shelter, in our garden ahead.
The dark sky was swept by the searchlights above,
     as the air raid sirens roared.
The enemy planes with their heavy bombs would dive, then they soared.

In the shelter we played games or slept.
Often people just sat and wept.
Their loved ones were so far away
And they prayed that they'd come home one day.
When we came out and looked around,
Rubble and damage was what we found.
In the big shelter that crossed two main streets,
Destruction and death we had to meet.
Almost four hundred, they did perish.
We learned that this war was really hellish.
For we never knew from day after day,
If it ever would ever go away.

There was sadness, heartache, always strife
In ours and all our neighbours' lives.
One thing we knew: that way out there,
Our war veterans had far more than their share.
They fought and fought with all their might,
To protect their families every night.
We stuck together, through thick and thin,
Then sang the songs of Vera Lynn,
"The White Cliffs of Dover" and "We'll Meet Again."
Then our tears we'd replace with a neat little grin.
After many years, soldiers, sailors and airman too
Came home to try and live anew.
The greatest thing no one could hide
Was the love we felt and the greatest pride.
On Remembrance Day, with this love and pride,
My heart goes out to those who died.

After the War

Though the war ended in 1945, rationing remained until the early '50s. But it was so nice to see other things return, like entertainment. Mum and I began to go to the pictures, or movies, as we call them now. We loved the new colour films, especially musicals. Dance halls opened up, and we began to see more sweets and fresh fruit. Overall, things were changing for the better.

Dad was leaving the Navy for good after twenty-two years, and Mum thought it was time for us to find our own place again. It would be strange after living with Grandma for nine years. Mum found a nice terrace house in Flinton Grove, two streets away from Grandma and next door to Aunt Edna and my cousins Brian and Frank, who were back from Halifax. Brian was old enough to start work, so we didn't see a lot of each other, but Frank was my age and inclined to be a real mischief. Our toilets were outside in the yard, and we both loved singing. If we were both out there, we would sing at the top of our voices and have loud conversations over the back wall. Needless to say, Mum did not think that was very ladylike, but we had some good laughs.

Iris still lived with Gran, Aunt Ivy and Uncle Ted. She came over often, and we still went to church together. I went round every day to play with Ann and saw Grandma after school. We often had sleepovers or dressed up and had concerts in the backyard. Toys were scarce in those days, but we still found ways to occupy our time, like listening to the radio.

We had a cat called Bonnie, who was so gentle. Once when Dad was home he found me a nice box on wheels and the old top from a doll's pram. He nailed them together and I had the best pram in the world. I would dress the cat in my old baby gown. She loved being pushed around and slept there all day. Later Bonnie had six kittens. The black one seemed to be dead, so Dad put it in the dustbin. A few hours later, it was found tottering around the bin. They were all cute. I wanted to keep them forever, but I knew that wouldn't be possible. One day I came home to find them all gone. I was heartbroken. Mum said a kind neighbour had taken them to her friends' farm. When I discovered the truth, I was revolted. Dad had actually drowned them one by one in a bucket of water. I didn't know if I could ever forgive that lie.

• • •

The time came to change schools. Ann would no longer be my schoolmate, but we would still meet up at weekends or after school at Grandma's. St. George's School was small but nice. It was a bit farther away, but I could get there by bike or bus. I liked the teachers and made another lifelong friend, Joyce. Her mum and dad owned a fruit stall in the marketplace downtown. I loved going there and smelling the lovely oranges, apples, pears and huge peaches that we hadn't seen during the war. We couldn't afford much, but at least now we had a choice. When Dad had come back from Africa, he'd brought a big stick of green bananas. Mum kept them in the cupboard next to the fireplace, where the warmth helped to ripen them. Three of us shared one banana.

One day Joyce and I went into our classroom to see a huge stack of boxes and tall tins lining the shelves. Our teacher explained that we had been sent a gift from Canada – boxes of apples and tins of apple juice. The labels had a picture of Mounties in red uniforms riding horses and carrying the Canadian flag. Though I had seen Nelson Eddie wearing a Mountie uniform, I hadn't realized it was such a beautiful, bright red — the films were always in black and white. We were all very excited. I said, "The Canadians are kind to send all this. They're so lucky to live in Canada," never having an inkling that many years later Canada would be my home too.

Weekends were shopping days, and the buses were full of factory girls. They would dress up in their best clothes, ready to go dancing or to the clubs, but they often still had their hair in curlers. Downtown there were some very good shops and a market to spend their wages in. There were huge red-and-white striped tents where we savoured fish and chips, along with mushy peas, splattered with dark malt vinegar.

Dad had left the Navy by then, and his wide-striped, navy blue demob suit was quite a ghastly shock after his nice military uniform.

It put me off stripes for the rest of my life. He landed a job in a chemical factory, working on the boilers as he had in the Navy's engine rooms, and settled in very well. A few months later he met Harry, another ex-sailor off his ship. Harry's daughter Maureen took ballet and tap lessons, and the company where she trained also did pantomimes, which were very popular in England, especially at Christmastime. It wasn't long before they convinced my parents to have me participate. I was very shy, and it took some time to convince me. Once I did it, however, I realized it was the best thing I could ever have done. I was a totally different person. I had independence I had never known before.

It was good to go somewhere on my own without my mother accompanying me. I enjoyed going on two long bus rides each way. I felt older and much more confident. I liked ballet, but I thought tap dancing was absolutely terrific. I was surprised how much I liked meeting people, also, considering how shy I had been. When I sang and danced, I really came out of myself. I was given the part of the Chief Fairy, Silver Wings, in the next pantomime, and many people came to see me, including Ann and her family.

To earn pocket money — one shilling, or twelve pence, a week — I cleaned the downstairs of the house, did all the dishes and windows, and tidied the small front garden. Mum often had asthma and bronchitis attacks, and I was pleased when she told me I could earn another sixpence if I did the upstairs as well. I happily got down on my knees and scrubbed the floors, then dusted and polished everything. We didn't have fitted carpets, just linoleum with rugs. While I was cleaning, I would sing at the top of my voice all the war songs and movie musicals I had seen.

School, meanwhile, was going well. We learned dressmaking and how to darn. It took a while to finish something, though, since there were thirty-eight of us sharing two machines. Once a week we could choose to do anything, and I did knitting or embroidery. We cooked in the mornings and learned table etiquette, then were shown how to wash and iron in the afternoons. The laundry began with a man's handkerchief, going up to a shirt in later weeks. It was considered very important to be able to run your own home properly after leaving school.

As we grew older, Joyce and I were allowed to go to the pictures on our own. We mostly went to musicals like *May Time*, starring my aforementioned favourite, Nelson Eddie, as a Mountie, with Jeanette Macdonald dressed in beautiful gowns. Jane Powell was another star who often sang with her. Howard Keel and Kathryn Grayson had such beautiful voices, too. We also saw war films starring John Wayne and

Jane Wyman. We loved her in *Johnny Belinda* and *Miracle in the Rain*. I thought we had cried a lot in *Lassie Come Home*, but we sobbed our hearts out in that one. That night we went back to Joyce's house with our eyes very red. Joyce's mum asked us what was wrong. We told her the picture had been sad, and while explaining, we both began crying again. One look at us and she said, "You silly buggers. Have a cup of tea and you'll both feel better." This was the English remedy for any problem.

Joyce and I didn't have any boyfriends, and we would sometimes giggle if boys stared at us. We looked to see if they were clean, because during the war some had dirty ears, holes in their elbows and socks that needing darning — sad, because with the time we spent running to the shelters day and night, there was little time to darn a few clothes. We didn't really seem to have any interest at all in boys until a new girl from Cambridge joined us. We heard so many stories about boys from her that we soon became very interested. Later when I went to Gran's house and saw Arnold, our next-door neighbour, I seemed to look at him in a different kind of way.

Joyce's two oldest brothers were in the Air Force, and the oldest one always seemed to catch my attention. Suddenly every time I saw him, my heart started to bump. What the heck was wrong with me? Every time I knocked on their door, I prayed he would be the one to open it, or at least be in the house. I suddenly realized he must be my first crush.

The first I had learned of periods was just after I was ten, when four of us settled down in the playground to hear a story from one of the girls, who said we would soon know when we were grown-up women. One day, she said, we would go into the toilet and our pee would turn red. Much later, as we were going out to a reunion of Dad's old Navy friends, Mum said to me, "If you see any blood between your legs while we're away, you mustn't mention it in front of the men." I had my first period during a music lesson at school, just after I turned twelve. I doubled over and the pain continued until I got home. Mum sent me to the chemist's for sanitary towels. She told me how to use them and said it would be best if I stayed away from boys for a while. I didn't understand why.

At twelve, I sat examinations to go to high school. I was happy when I found I had passed the scholarship to go to the art school or the high school, with special courses to enter nursing later on. As long as I could remember, I had wanted to be a nurse, though there was a spell when I thought I might try window dressing in the large stores. After an interview and a tour of the art school, I decided there was too much sewing, painting and embroidery involved. I chose to take the nursing course at Thoresby High School. There I would be able to concentrate on the sciences and subjects relevant to nursing. They also trained students to become teachers or to go into other professions. Those students were taught typing and shorthand and French, a subject I would have liked but that sadly wasn't on our list.

I knew I wouldn't be able to earn money like my friends or go dancing with them. I would have to struggle by on pocket money. I would certainly miss my friends. I decided instead to take a first aid course and joined the Saint John's Ambulance. I was allowed to volunteer at the Children's Hospital, where I helped feed the babies in the burns ward. What a terrible sight, to see little toddlers and tiny babies covered head to toe in burns. At first I thought the nurses seemed a little bit hard — I guess I expected to see them cuddling the babies constantly. Impossible, of course. It didn't take me long to realize that to deal with those kinds of sights every day, it takes a very special person with a very special stance. I knew right away that if I did go for nursing, I might be too sensitive to work constantly in this area. I kept feeling like adopting them all and taking them home with me. Stupid even to think that, but I guess that is all part of caring. The more I saw, the more my admiration for those nurses grew.

The worst part of all this was changing schools and having to leave Joyce behind.

High School

I knew it was going to be difficult for my parents to buy my new school uniform, so I tried to save any money I could. I found most of what I needed at the uniform store — a gymslip (jumper dress) with a blue belt, a tie, a blazer, a raincoat and a hat — except my white drip-dry shirts. Mum found me a cheaper cream-coloured shirt with cardboard buttons.

At twelve, I really didn't know much about rich and poor. I thought everyone had to work hard for everything. All the people around us were the same. Though food had been rationed for years, we all seemed to eat well. Yet I do remember that when there wasn't enough, parents ate a lot less than their children. We all wore the same uniform in school, so no one could tell rich from poor. But those shirts started me thinking, and I began to ask myself why I couldn't be like the others. There were only a few of us with cardboard buttons, which when washed went soft and rusty.

Everyone where I lived rented their homes or lived in a council house. The odd person with a business we assumed had a bit more money, yet the Halls, who had the little grocery store down our street, seemed like very ordinary and hardworking people. Our local newsagents, on the other hand, gave the impression that they were somehow better than anyone else. The man was friendly, but the wife had a tendency to boast over silly little things, especially about her daughter going to high school. Her face changed a little when my mum mentioned that I had passed my scholarship and was going to the same school. I don't doubt she was as proud as my own mum. At my high school I met girls whose parents owned their houses and cars, which was quite rare in those days.

My mum seemed to be different from everyone else in our family. Not that she was full of airs and graces, as most of them thought. At fourteen, she went on a visit to her father's family in Norfolk and saw an altogether different lifestyle. They were well off, wealthy compared to where she lived. They had a servant, ate from tureens and changed into another dress for each meal. They were well educated and didn't use any bad language, as people did around the docks. Mum recognized it as a better life and wanted hers to be the same. Her brothers would try to take the mickey out of her when she reprimanded them for swearing. They would laugh and then try to tempt me. "Call your mum a bugger and we'll give you a tanner." Wow, that was sixpence! Had I done what they asked, I could have been a millionaire by now.

But a tongue-less millionaire, had my mother heard me. She used to brandish a big carving knife and say, "If you ever repeat those words, I'll cut your tongue out with this." Also "If you ever get yourself into trouble, I'll stick this through you." I tried to figure out what she meant by "getting into trouble." Her other favourite threat was that if I ever smoked a cigarette, she would put the lit end down my throat. As a child, it was good to be on my best behaviour all the time.

• • •

One day Uncle Charlie popped in to ask Gran and Uncle Ted which horse they wanted to bet on. Nobody could decide. Charlie said, "Come and help us, Patsy. Pick a winner for us and if it wins, we'll treat you." So he read out the list. My ears pricked up when he said White Heather, and the sad story of Aunt Ivy and George came back to me.

Aunt Ivy was always like a second mother to Iris and me. She had been a tomboy when she was young, and her favourite games were marbles and cigarette cards. She wore waistcoats and baggy pants like the boys. When older, she enjoyed playing cards in the local club and, with the rest of the family, betting on horses.

It seemed she was quite lucky in winning prizes but unlucky in her love life. After becoming a bus conductor, she met George, a very nice soldier. He was in the Scottish regiment known as the Black Watch, whose uniforms included beautiful dark green kilts. He knew I was shy, and he used to pretend to be a tiger and chase me under the kitchen table. He was really nice and we were all happy when we heard they were planning to get married after the war. But it was not meant to be. In Burma he was captured by the Japanese and tortured in a prison camp. Somehow he managed to escape and tried to get back to his camp, but unfortunately he died.

While planning their wedding, George and Aunt Ivy had mentioned that Scottish white heather was lucky, and they had intended to put some in their Bible for the ceremony. Now it was as if something told me the horse White Heather would be lucky. Uncle Charlie, Gran and Uncle Ted all put a shilling on it each way. Later, back came Uncle Charlie to tell us White Heather was the winner. Wow! Between them I was given twelve shillings and sixpence, more money than I had ever had. I needed a new pair of shoes that Mum couldn't afford at the time, so that's what I bought. Needless to say, out came the cobbler's last, and Mum sat on the floor as usual, hammering studs around the heels and soles.

• • •

I loved my new school and teachers. During debates, I lost my shyness and was able to join in. I joined field hockey and swimming and went to football games at weekends. I felt I was coming out of my shell. Beryl, who was crazy about sailing ships, got me to join the Sea Rangers, along with another friend, Ann. Jokingly, I said to Mum and Dad that I might decide to join the Wrens (Women's Royal Naval Service). "Over my dead body!" Dad said. I thought that, having been in the Navy so long, he maybe knew a lot about them, more than he would say. I decided not to ask.

Once a month students at my school were able to go to the theatre for two shillings, a reasonable price. We were introduced to some beautiful classical music, opera and ballet. Aunt Ivy took me to *Swan Lake*. Joyce and I still went to the pictures in our spare time, and my heart still bumped at the sight of her brother. I guess we were really growing up. I felt happy.

Then Mum and Grandma had a falling out which left me devastated. Gran swore at Mum and Mum told her to "wash your mouth out with disinfectant and soapy water." This would end their relationship for sixteen years. I was panic-stricken, my mind in a whirl. What was going to happen without our Grandma, Aunt Ivy and Uncle Ted? We were a family. What about Iris? She was the only sister I had ever had.

Things were a little awkward at times, but I was always allowed to visit. I went to Gran's after school most days. When Mum baked apple pies, she would give me one to take to Gran. Every spring when wallflowers came out we would buy a bunch for Gran, as they had always been her favourite flower. As the years went by, I found the situation between Mum and Gran ridiculous and very sad. Here were two people who had always loved one another dearly, yet both were too stubborn to forgive each other and apologize. I was to see this kind of thing happen to others in our family years later.

• • •

Dad's job at the chemical plant involved both shift work and a long commute. As a result, I did not see much of him and could keep out of his way. I understood instinctively that I needed to be careful. By this point, I knew of his perverted predilections, the sick, twisted arousal he derived from touching me, bouncing me on his knee and exposing himself to me. My hope was that it would end there. For if it continued, I had nobody to tell.

Unfortunately it was not to stop there. He suggested that if I was nice to him and did some things he wanted, I would be rewarded with anything I asked for. It would be our very own secret. Later came exposing himself, saying what he had to give me and how I would enjoy it. I was disgusted and frightened. What to do? All I was certain of was that it was very wrong. If I told Mum, what would happen? Would she believe me, blame me or kill me? I was literally terrified at the thought.

Dad said that years ago in Kent I had taken a lot of pleasure from knee bouncing and the odd little touch he gave me. I tried to think back. I had just turned seven then and was getting to know my dad for the first time. Had that fun been in some way sexual? My thoughts then went back to the very first time we had all been together. I was three years old. The four-poster bed on the trip to Scotland — could there have been the odd touch then? Did I have a faint recollection that now and again my nighty kept sliding up? It all went round in my mind. Could it just be my imagination? Why was this happening to me? This was someone I had always loved, even when he was just a photo to me during his years in the Navy. How was I going to cope with all this? I dared not tell anyone. My nightmare had begun.

His behaviour confused me. The most I knew about sex was the dirty little jokes I had heard at school, which we just giggled about. I was to learn much, much more. Every now and again he would tell me stories, almost as if he needed someone to talk to or confide in. It was as if he felt safe to tell me because he knew I would never dare repeat any of it. I was much too shy and too scared to tell anyone. Maybe it was a way for him to get rid of his guilt.

One story was that when he was growing up there were many large families, and sisters and brothers had to share beds. It was quite common, he said, for the boys to experiment on their sisters, touching them or actually having sex. This got me to wondering why his sister didn't speak to him anymore. Another story concerned men in the forces who spent many years abroad and would often go to prostitutes for sex. In several places he was stationed, there were young boys on the streets selling their little sisters for sex. I had a horrible feeling that this may have been his preference. He might have felt less guilty about breaking his marriage vows by going with a child instead of an adult. Perhaps less chance of disease, too. He also told me about a sex show he went to while he was abroad. Most of it was with young girls, he said. He told me how a wine bottle was inserted into a fourteen-year-old girl and she had sighed with pleasure.

It was obvious to me that he had been excited by doing these things in secret. In his mind he was hoping to do them with me. Well, he was going to be disappointed. I was a child, but boy was I learning fast! Child or not, I knew I could never go along with anything like that. It was totally wrong. Why was he doing this to my mother? They had always seemed so much in love. What would she do if she ever found out? I couldn't bear to think about it.

A Baby Sister

One day out of the blue, Mum told us she was expecting a baby. I was surprised but happy. I had missed having Iris around, and here I was going to have my very own little sibling. Dad had always wanted a son named David. Grandma's reaction, however, was not good. "It's disgusting at her age," she remarked to a friend. Mum was thirty-seven. Some said I would get my nose pushed out when the baby arrived, which I still think was a cruel thing to say to a child. I have since always made a point, when I buy a gift for a new baby, to also buy one for its siblings so they don't feel left out.

I worried about Mum's frequent attacks of asthma and bronchitis and wondered how she would cope with a new baby. But there was always me to help, as I was about to find out. As Mum's asthma got worse, and the cupboard filled with cough mixture and tablets, I found myself taking on more jobs at home. I missed so many swimming classes that I had to give up taking my Bronze Medal. I never did get a chance to take it again.

• • •

Dad's worrisome advances, touching and exposure did not stop. Seeing little of him due to his shift work and commutes did not mean that he was out of my life altogether. For some reason I had thought it would go away, that a new baby in the house would change things. No such luck. Quite the opposite, in fact, as I would find out. My father was a pedophile who needed to satisfy his deranged desires. I spent every minute I could hidden in my room. I practised on my cash register, playing shops. I wrote poetry and read, anything to take my mind off his extremely unsettling behaviour.

One day I went to my room and found a long poem on my dresser in Dad's handwriting, telling me how lovely I was and talking about my body. I read it in horror. What could I do? I wanted to scream. My first thought was that this was evidence of what had been going on. I ran as fast as I could to find Joyce. I had to tell someone, and she was the only one I could trust. Joyce was shocked, but even together we had no idea what to do. Our concern was the same – what was going to happen if the family found out? Especially Mum, in her present state. There seemed to be no answer, but I felt better just knowing that Joyce and I had talked about it. I knew it would stay between us.

I went home intending to read the poem again and then hide it. But it was gone. I searched every drawer. I should have taken it with me. I should have known he would go into my room to find it. I asked him what he had done with his poem. Smiling, he said, "You don't think I'd risk leaving something like that around, do you?" I felt totally lost and stupid. I couldn't prove anything now.

After that came the threats — I should do what he wanted or he would get friendly with my girlfriends. Now I was scared to bring anyone home with me. The next time we were at the swimming pool, I saw he was being extra friendly with one of my friends, almost flirting with her. At the same time, he gave me a nice smile. A smile I didn't like. It made me shudder.

Though I spent most of my time at home in my room, if I had to be around Mum and Dad I buried my head in a book. If I was asked to put the kettle on for tea, I would light the gas ring with one hand still holding my book. They scolded me for that, telling me my reading was becoming an obsession. I read in bed till after midnight, so they replaced my light bulb with the tiniest one they could find. It was very hard on my eyes. Dad seemed to enjoy this punishment, saying I was using too much electricity.

He used to try to torment me while he helped Mum do the washing. We didn't have a washing machine, so he would sit on the bottom of the staircase and put his feet in the tub of water, as they did in the Navy. Every time I went into the kitchen, he would get out my panties and slowly rub the crotch. I was furious.

Sometimes when Mum was out, he would grab me and try to hold me down on the table. Then he'd pull open the leg of my underwear and try to touch me. I fought and kicked till he let me go; his boxing lessons came in very handy. The more I fought him, the meaner he got. I only had to say Oh! to Mum and he would slap me across the face or head — for answering her back, so he said.

One day after school Mum asked me to go for groceries. When I got back, the butter they'd given me was three pennies more than she wanted to pay. I went back to the store, but the butter she wanted was out of stock — hence they had given me the other. I was angry when I came home again, and I said, "All that way for nothing!" Dad gave me a slap across the face. "Don't talk to your mother that way," he said.

It almost knocked me over, and I ran to the stairs to get out of the way. Unfortunately, he came after me, saying, "You're not going to hide up there." I almost made it to the top, but he caught my jacket and dragged me, face down, down every step. The stairs in the kitchen had a door, and I banged my shoulders and back on the doorknob.

Dad started hitting me hard across my face and head. Mum said, "That's enough!" but he didn't stop. Scared, she picked up a plate and threw it to distract him. Unfortunately, it hit him. Mum said she was sorry but she thought he had gone too far. She just didn't know what had got into him. Pity I couldn't tell her the real reason.

The next day I was bruised all over. I ached everywhere, and my forehead and face were black and blue. I was scared to go to school, but I decided I would tell my friends I had fallen down the stairs, an accident. When I walked past my teacher's desk, she smiled and said, "I hate to tell you, Pat, but you have quite a dirty face. You look as if you've been in a chimney." I tried to laugh, and told her it was bruises from falling down the stairs the night before. I crossed my fingers behind my back and pretended I was telling a little white lie. I still didn't want to hurt anyone. My teacher apologized.

• • •

The baby was due anytime. A second child would bring with it major costs. I checked my Post Office stamp book, because Mum said she might have to borrow it. There was fifteen pounds in there, saved for college. I knew our baby would need the money more than I would need it for college, so I drew it out and gave it to Mum.

During the birth I stayed with our neighbours, as Dad was on night shift. I was very pleased to be in their house instead of alone in ours with my dad. After a few days, Dad came home from the hospital to tell us he had another daughter. I was so excited. I thought this would be the best and happiest day of our lives. Instead it turned out to be the worst night of my life.

I was fast asleep at home, literally exhausted from excitement, when I suddenly became aware of feeling funny. I realized my nighty was up and my legs were wide open. I was being touched, and someone's head was under the covers. In shock, I cried out to be left alone. Dad said he needed me to come to his big bed. He would be very gentle with me. The time had come to do things together. When we had done it, I would love it and want more. He said I could be his other wife and he would buy me lots of fancy underwear or anything I wanted. I couldn't stop crying for him to leave me alone. I sobbed and sobbed, so scared I couldn't stop.

After a while, he suddenly fell on his knees and cried out for God to help him stop what he was doing. I was stunned, because he had always said he was an atheist, that he didn't believe in God. Yet I remembered him saying that when his ship was blown up everyone had called for God's help in the water. Well, God must have heard his call that night. Suddenly he left the room and I was alone. I was scared for a while that he might come back, and worried about what he would do to me if he did. He didn't come back, and I thanked God myself.

I was amazed, however, at my own feelings. I was so tired of fighting, I was almost ready to give in. I was at the point where if Dad had come back, I might have said, "Just do what you want to do." I knew I couldn't have fought anymore. The next morning, I was so pleased that I hadn't given in to him. I was sure God had stepped in to help me. I was aware now of these different feelings, but I also knew it was very wrong to give in and always would be. I knew in my heart that God would always be there to give me the strength I needed to keep on fighting. I also knew in my heart that this would not be the end.

That morning I ran all the way to Grandma's. I didn't know what I was feeling — excited about my baby sister, scared about what had happened the previous night and apprehensive about what was about to happen with the baby routine. There were so many thoughts going through my mind. As I ran down the street, I saw Gran outside talking to her friend. In my excitement I shouted out, "Gran, I've got a new daughter!" They smiled, and then Gran's face changed to a frown. Little did I realize that my sister would become more like a daughter.

In those days only the father was allowed to visit the hospital, so I was very happy when they finally came home and I met my little sister. Another redhead joined the family. Unlike my hair, hers was a golden colour, and her eyes were a pretty blue. Mum asked if there were any names I liked. "Barbara," I said, the same name as my ballet and tap teacher. Both Mum and Dad liked it. Six weeks later I was dressing her up for her christening. I was hoping with all my heart that now Barbara was with us, everything would change for the better.

The Miscarriage

On the bus to school, I was given my first love letter. Ken, a boy from another high school, said he liked me and asked if he could take me to the pictures. I was still quite timid. We had been on the same bus a long time, but I had never noticed him before. I began to talk to him, and after a while I agreed to go out. We met at the pictures and he gave me a box of Cadbury's chocolates. He held my hand and gave me a quick goodnight kiss as we walked home.

The next week as I went into the schoolyard, a blonde girl came hurrying towards me, her fist raised as if she was about to hit me. I hadn't a clue who she was. I was flabbergasted when she screamed at me, "You devil, you've pinched my boyfriend!"

"What?" I asked.

"Ken," she said. "He's mine!"

I told her I'd had no idea he was going out with someone else and she was welcome to keep him. A week later I was quite nervous when I saw her walking towards me again, smiling.

"I thought I'd tell you I've dropped Ken," she said. "I'm going out with a new fellow." Thank goodness we weren't in the same class.

Iris found a boyfriend and they began to go out regularly. Aunt Ivy said "Sixteen is too young," and she and Iris argued. In the end, Iris decided to leave Grandma's house and go home to her parents. She stopped coming to church, and we only heard how she was from friends. Before we knew it, news came that she was getting married. I knew our family wouldn't be going. They held too many grudges. I never knew anything about her wedding, her husband or where they lived. It would be many, many years before I saw her again.

Things were getting busier at home. With Mum's problematic health, I seemed to be getting more and more jobs to do. I had to get up extra early in the mornings to get Barbara ready for Mum before I left. Some days I would tuck her in her pram and go to the butcher's to get some meat for dinner. Or we would go to the bakery to buy some hotcakes.

I had quite a laugh one morning on my errands when two older ladies remarked to the butcher, "How sad to see these young wives have to bring their babies out so early on these cold mornings." The butcher looked at me and smiled. He was a classmate of Mum's, so he knew Barbara was my sister. At fourteen, I looked more like seventeen. On weekends the butcher boy, who was very handsome, would ride his bike alongside the pram when he was delivering. It was nice to be escorted home. I hoped he might ask me out.

When Barbara was eight months old, Dad began to look very worried. I asked him if anything was wrong, and he told me something no one must know — Mum was pregnant again. What a shock! He said, "There's no way she can cope with another baby. She just isn't well enough." He told me he was going to the chemist's to get some pills that might help change things.

I couldn't believe what he was saying. If someone got pregnant out of wedlock, they were sent to another town to hide the shame and the babies were adopted or got rid of. Having sex before marriage was a real no-no. I had heard of backstreet abortions, usually done with knitting needles. Or if you missed a period, sometimes drinking large amounts of gin would correct it. The result, I'd heard, was often hemorrhages or death.

Dad said again that he would love to have a son but that Mum would never be able to handle it. I had noticed Mum getting sullen, and now I knew why. I couldn't say anything to her about it, as I wasn't supposed to know. I just tried to take care of Babs more, to make it a little easier for her. I did tell Dad that Mum seemed to be more depressed. A few days later he came downstairs to find her with her head in the gas oven. Thank God she was found before any real damage was done. Dad begged her not to do it ever again. I wanted to call the doctor, but Mum said she just wanted to rest. I decided to stay off school again to look after Babs while Mum was in bed.

I'd been home three days. Mum was still in bed and Babs was asleep. I was washing the dishes, when I suddenly heard Mum calling for help. I ran upstairs to find her on the potty, very breathless. She was trying to get into bed but kept falling over. I pulled back the sheets and found they were soaked in blood. I managed to get her on the bed, intending to clean her up, but first I had to move the potty. There was something strange in there, like a teeny rubber doll, floating in blood. It had what looked like facial marks and little arms. I felt scared. Could this be my baby brother?

I did all I could to clean her up, but the bleeding didn't stop and I was frightened. Mum was as white as a ghost. Dad came in early, and I asked him to go and phone for an ambulance. We had no private phones and the public one was quite a walk away, but luckily there was a tiny grocer's at the end of our terrace. Dad used their phone, and the ambulance came quickly. Mum was hemorrhaging. She was in hospital a while, and it was touch and go. All that was said was she'd had a miscarriage, and it was never spoken of again. It was clear Mum could never have coped with another child.

Growing Up

Life went on, and I went back to school again. Our church was having a dance, my first one ever. When I asked Mum about staying out late at the dance with my friend Betty, the answer was an emphatic no. Ann and my friends who had already left school went to the Scala Dancing Hall every week, but Mum said the girls who went to those places were cheap and looking for men. I asked her why I couldn't go to the church dance, as it would be different. "It's not the dance," she replied, "it's what happens after."

Mum said I could go to the dance if Dad picked me up after work. Oh boy, I thought, if she knew what I knew! I would be far safer on the bus than with him on his bike. I told Mum that if they couldn't trust me now, with all my responsibilities at home, volunteering in the hospital, and helping at the church, then I wouldn't go under any circumstances. I was deeply hurt. I gave up going to church and decided to do what I enjoyed, Sea Rangers and going to the pictures with Joyce or Betty.

At fifteen I was at last able to wear a blouse and skirt at school. The gymslips didn't look too good when your breasts started to develop. I was also able to choose my own shoes for the first time. I picked a pair of navy blue wedge pumps with suede tops and leather heels, and I said goodbye to all the studs. The shoes matched my skirt perfectly, and I felt I was finally becoming a woman.

My next new clothes came at Easter. That was usually our time to buy new clothes or shoes, if we could afford them; if not, we tried six weeks later at Whitsuntide, the next annual holiday. Because of my red hair Mum had always dressed me in green, and I was tired of it. When she mentioned she had found a good dressmaker I said, "Please, Mum, could

I have something in mustard or teal blue?" Easter came and she gave me a parcel. I held my breath and opened it slowly, praying to God it wasn't green. I saw a lovely mustard shade. How wonderful! It would certainly enhance the colour of my hair. It was a suit — a neat jacket with a pleated skirt — something I had never had before.

Things were changing for sure. Mum found a house for us in Bilton Grange, across the city. It was two bus rides each way to school, but I didn't care. Dad was not too far from his work. For the first time we had a home with hot water and a bathroom. We also had our own rooms. What more could we wish for?

Before, Iris, Ann and I had always come in to Gran's house by seven o'clock to listen to the radio. We listened to *Dick Barton, Special Agent*; the Paul Temple detective series; *The Archers*, the world's longest-running radio soap opera, which still airs today; *Variety*, on which Wilfred Pickles played the piano for popular singers and we would all join in; and the scary voice of Valentine Dyall, a.k.a. The Man in Black. Saturdays we all went to the matinees and saw cowboy and Indian films — Tom Mix, Gene Autry, Roy Rogers and his famous horse Trigger, and later, the Lone Ranger and Tonto.

Now it was strange at the pictures without Iris. I wondered how she was finding running her own home. Ann and Joyce were both working. Yes, we were growing up, and we had to adapt to new lives. Mum, Dad, Babs and I all settled well into our new house, but I was feeling extremely tired.

We hadn't lived there long when I was introduced through friends to Neville. He seemed quiet but nice, very nice. He was a marine engineer, training in the Merchant Navy. He asked if he could walk me home. We began to meet often, walking or going to the pictures, but he never said very much. He seemed to enjoy my company, so I thought he must be shy like me.

Aunt Ivy was now a manager at the bus canteen, and when I visited her there I chatted a lot with the drivers. I had known a couple of the conductors for years, having ridden the buses for so long. One of the ones who flirted with me was married. The other one was a bit older than me, but I really liked him. I mentioned to my parents that he had asked me out, and Dad was angry. He asked why a man that age would want to take me out unless he wanted something. Mum told him, "That's enough, Alf." Then to me she said, "He is a bit old for you." I did go for a walk with him now and again, and to the pictures. Mum was right, though – he was too old for me.

At a jamboree with the River Scouts, we were sitting on the floor in a circle with candles in the middle, singing songs, when suddenly someone grabbed my hand. Till the lights went on, I couldn't see who it was. I was rather annoyed, but he introduced himself as David. We had both come by bike, so he asked if he could ride home with me. Neville hadn't been able to come that night, and I didn't see any harm in it, so I thought, why not?

I was too bothered about what was going on at home to go out with anyone, really. The next weekend I was to go out with Neville, but I couldn't bring myself to go. I decided to run to the phone box and ring him. I told him I was behind on studying and not feeling well. A lie. Then suddenly I said, "I don't think we should see each other again. We don't talk very much, anyway." I said I was sorry and that was that. He just gasped. I hung up and had a good cry. I felt so bad. He was a nice person.

David kept asking me to come over to his home, and quite a while later I agreed. Most of the time, he was in his darkroom developing pictures, and after a while I was bored stiff. Even his mum suggested he take me out to the pictures or go to the park across the road. He gave me a few kisses, but I felt nothing. I began to regret that I had stopped going out with Neville. I'd blown that one myself. Yet in my mind, I knew I shouldn't be going out with anyone. It seemed I was losing interest in everything.

• • •

It had been quiet with Dad, except for his habit of exposing himself as we passed each other near the bathroom. I ignored what he was doing and he gave me some very nasty looks. Those I could take, but I was always on edge wondering what he might get up to next, and worrying that Mum would see him doing something. I couldn't trust him anymore. I was glad Mum and Babs were around more.

One afternoon when I came home from school, the house seemed exceedingly quiet. No sign of anyone. I hung up my coat and headed for the kitchen to make some tea. Suddenly I was grabbed by Dad, who had been waiting behind the door. He dragged me to the folded table and pinned me down. He began pulling the elastic leg on my panties. He yelled that he was going to have me and he should have done it years ago.

As usual I kicked and screamed back at him to leave me alone. I was trapped on the narrow table and couldn't get away. I felt so helpless. What right had he to invade my privacy and touch my body? Mum had always said, "Never say the word *hate* to anyone or think it." At that moment I really hated him. I struck out as hard as I could with my fists and anything I could use. He couldn't keep me down. At last I got away, and I ran upstairs and locked my door. I put my chair under the doorknob — anything to keep him out. It wasn't long before I heard Mum come in with Babs. I was safe then, but this latest episode had me on edge for some time.

Another day after I had showered, I went to get clean underwear from my drawer. Everything seemed rumpled, so I began to fold my panties up. Suddenly I noticed a funny smell and saw stains on the crotches. It was semen. Every pair was the same. My head began to spin. I was disgusted and sick with worry. Oh God, whatever would he do next? All that week he kept giving me sickly smiles. I felt like spitting in his face. I just wished I could run away. I wanted to be by myself. I was terrified of Mum finding out. The next week I told Betty how tired I was. I didn't want to go to school or do anything. Our friend Brenda suggested, "Why don't all three of us just do that?" We met up the very next day downtown. We walked through the market, spent time in the old church, had lunch, and visited our famous museum, the house of William Wilberforce. We had agreed that if anyone asked, we would say we were doing a project for school. I guess they were used to students being around in uniform, because nobody asked.

It didn't worry me in the least that I had played truant from school. I had thoroughly enjoyed it, and Betty and I did it again a few weeks later. This time we went to the pictures, out of uniform and without a thought that it was wrong. I just didn't care anymore. The way I was feeling, it was the best thing I could have done. I felt I badly needed a rest, and I had this terrible urge to get away. I kept praying to God to send me away somewhere, anywhere.

I was now in my last phase of high school, so college wasn't far away. One day when I'd popped over to Ann's, the neighbours' door opened and out came Arnold. We had played together since we were tots, but now when I looked at him my heart went bump. I had never noticed how handsome he was before.

"I rarely see you anymore since you moved," he said. "You look lovely in that turquoise dress. It really suits your red hair." I blushed as he took my hand and walked me into the alley next to his house. There he kissed me. Wow! "You've grown into such a lovely girl," he said. "Yes, you sure have grown. You better get some bras. Your nipples are showing through your dress."

I wanted to die on the spot. Here I was, sixteen with a thirty-six-inch bust, but Mum had never said anything about me wearing bras. When I got home I plucked up my courage and told her people had made remarks about my nipples. "Go into the sideboard," she said. "There's a pile of them in there." I found them all knotted up, and for over half an hour I sat on the floor trying to untangle them. A horrible pile of dark-beige bras, but they sure did the trick. Arnold asked me to come over for the Guy Fawkes bonfire on our old street. I couldn't wait to see him.

That night Ann and I looked everywhere for him, but he didn't turn up. Ann had told me earlier not to be disappointed if he didn't show. "He's been seen with a blonde who recently moved in here." Our friend Joan joined us, and we asked her if she had seen him. "Oh yes," she said. "He's in the house just up the road with the new girl. They're always up there when her mum's out. The bedroom lights are always on." I was upset, but couldn't say anything.

"She goes to Thoresby High," said Joan. "Don't you know her?" I hadn't a clue. The bonfires were dying down, and it was time to go catch my bus.

What was wrong with me? I wondered. I always felt the odd one out. Would it ever change? I said bye to Ann and Joan and strolled up the road. As I walked past the houses, a door opened and out came Arnold, followed by the blonde. "Oh no," I thought, "I don't believe this."

It was the same blonde who had raised her fist to me at school over Ken. I was stunned, but I managed to say, "Hello, hope you had a nice night?" Arnold looked a bit sheepish. Another lesson learned. I knew for sure any feelings I might have had for him were over. I never wanted to get tangled up with her again.

• • •

Mum was getting to know our neighbours, and Babs was getting cuter by the day. Dad was quieter than usual, so I was on guard and kept my eyes wide open. I would soon find out what he was up to. One day I came home to a very quiet house, so I checked carefully to see that he wasn't hiding anywhere. Then I had a drink and went upstairs to change my uniform.

My door was slightly open, so I peeped through the crack. Feeling there was someone in my bed, I held my breath. I knew where Mum and Barbara were. Dad's bike wasn't in the passageway, and Mum had said he wouldn't be home till late. I put my head around the door slowly. The bed was ruffled and the pillows were out of place. I thought Babs might have been jumping on my bed, yet the pillows were under the sheets and the wrong way around. I began to tidy up, pulling back the sheets, and saw my pyjamas had been stuffed with the pillows. It looked like a person lying with both legs wide apart. I could see a large patch of smelly semen all over the crotch and front of my pyjamas. I knew that, as with my underwear, he was showing me he was enjoying sex with my clothing.

I felt sick and scared stiff. He must have done this after Babs and Mum had gone. What would have happened if they had come home earlier and gone in there? I tidied it as quickly as I could, and I wept. This had to stop. There had to be something really wrong with him. It was so wrong to be doing all these things.

Conversely, when he hadn't done anything for a while, there couldn't have been a nicer person. I could talk to him better than I could to Mum. I noticed that when I went out with someone like Neville, he seemed fine for a while.

That night he came home at the same time as Mum and Babs. I didn't think I could look at him. I shouted hello from upstairs and said I would be down for tea after I had finished my homework. I felt so bad that I didn't want to eat anything. After I went down Mum noticed my eyes looked a bit red. I didn't look at Dad. I felt as if I was choking. I told them I didn't feel well, that I would rather go to bed.

I cried most of the night. Mum said, "Whatever is wrong with you?" I just couldn't stop crying. I carried on for two full days, and my eyes became red and puffy. On the third day Mum called the doctor. She told him they were very worried, that they had never seen me like this. The doctor tried to talk to me, but I was crying non-stop and didn't say a word. He said I was worn out and had been overdoing my studying. He left a prescription for medication, telling both my parents that I was very near a total breakdown.

I was in bed a full week before I felt rested. The doctor visited twice. I could see that both Mum and Dad were really worried, even frightened. They had a look of relief when I finally got out of bed. Strangely enough, Mum never asked me any questions. All I did was pray to God to get me away from all this.

Back at school I focused on my studying and my exams. In a few more weeks I would be leaving for good. I felt much happier and not so tired. I had a six-week holiday to look forward to. Then I would be in college.

A Trip to Norwich

I think God had been listening, because something unexpected happened. A letter arrived for Mum from Aunt Frances in Norwich, an hour northeast of London. This was the family Mum met when she was fourteen, the ones she said changed her life.

Aunt Frances was a nursing Matron who had worked abroad in Italy and other places, and the cousins had all become nursing Sisters. Over the years they kept in touch with Grandma, and after Gran told Aunt Frances I was going into nursing studies, she wrote and asked Mum if I would like to spend the summer holidays with them before I went to college. I couldn't believe someone, out of the blue, would ask me to spend six weeks with them. How happy I was! God alone knew how much I needed this break. He really had answered my prayers. I would never doubt again that He listened. For me it was a miracle.

Planning to keep myself busy while I was there, I bought some yellow wool to knit things for Barbara. I said my goodbyes on a foggy morning at the railway station and six hours later walked into nothing but sunshine. My aunt and uncle were both there to meet me. They brought me to their bungalow, a grand place with a long driveway. They obviously loved their garden — there were oval flower beds everywhere, surrounded by lavender. The perfume was magnificent.

Every day while Uncle Arthur pottered in the garden, Aunt Frances and I sat outside. We all read and talked non-stop. I had expected Aunt Frances, being a Matron, to be pretty strict. How wrong I was. She treated me like an adult. It crossed my mind that if I were around people like her more often, I might lose my terrible shyness. I felt relaxed now.

Mum had said they ate from tureens and had to change their dresses for each meal, but things had changed over the years. We didn't change our dresses unless we went out to dinner or to something special, though meals were eaten from tureens. I said I would wash all the dishes while I was there, which pleased Aunt Frances. The cutlery had to be washed first, in very hot soapy water, then rinsed and dried by slipping the cloth through every tine of every fork. The water was then thrown away and fresh water was used for the rest of the dishes. It did make sense, though it took a little bit longer.

Norwich had a huge marketplace with good shopping and a big cathedral. I met Olive, Aunt Frances's niece, and we went all over Norwich together. I was beginning to feel I could live there forever. Mum wrote and sent me pocket money, so I was able to buy some nice gifts to take home. While there was rain and thunder in the rest of England, the weather in Norwich was glorious.

One night we all went to the theatre. The showgirls were naked up top. I wondered what my aunt and uncle's reaction would be. I didn't have long to wait. As we left the theatre, Aunt Frances said, "What nice artists they were, and how beautiful their bodies were." They were not in the least narrow-minded.

We went to visit Aunt Frances's sisters in Yarmouth. Agnes was a nurse, married and with a family. Unfortunately her daughter had been disabled for years. In spite of the hard work, they were happy and loving people. We were very surprised when Frances's other sister Flo and her husband, both in their sixties, arrived on motorcycles. During the war, Flo's husband had been badly injured in the Air Force and was in the hospital for some time. Flo had been his ward Sister. After he'd recovered, they went out together and eventually married.

Aunt Frances told me about assisting the Mountbatten family in Spain. They had two daughters, Patricia and Pamela, and I believe it was Pamela's birth she assisted in. I saw the gold watch they gave her as a gift, engraved with their names. Their lady-in-waiting also gave her a gift, a long ivory necklace with matching earrings. It must have been quite an honour.

On my last night, Aunt Frances gave me a few white lab coats that I would be able to use in the college laboratory. She also gave me a shiny green square box with a white satin lining. I lifted the lid and held my breath when I saw what was in it – a long ivory necklace with matching earrings. Every bead was knotted individually. I couldn't believe this was going to belong to me.

Looking back on my stay afterwards, I realized they had done for me the same thing their family did for Mum all those years ago.

Back at home, I was ready to begin a new adventure. Kingston upon Hull College of Technology, here I came! My goal was to have obtained Part 1 of my Nursing Registration by the end of the following year, after which I would be able to enter the hospital as a student nurse. I felt I was on the right path, and I couldn't wait to get started.

Adulthood
1953 – 1967

College

College was different from anything I had ever done. I was sixteen now, an adult, and hard work lay ahead. The instructors we met on the first day were welcoming. Our medical instructor was from a large TB (tuberculosis) and mental hospital. He explained that later he would take us on a tour of all the local hospitals so we could choose where to do our training.

When we came to the Biology lab, a lady in a white coat was standing at the door, staring at us through thick horn-rimmed glasses. She didn't smile as she read out our names. Her eyes scanned the room and came to rest on me, which made me very nervous. In a loud voice she said, "Hey you, Marmalade! I couldn't remember your name, but your lovely hair made me think of a nice jar of marmalade." Her face changed to a beaming smile and we both burst out laughing. I had been called many names — Bluey (Australian slang for redhead), Ginger, Carrots, Red, and Rusty (which I didn't mind; it matched both my hair and my deep voice) — but Marmalade was new. From that moment, I knew we would all get on well together. She had a terrific sense of humour.

There was a tuck shop next to the college where we went for tea breaks and to meet with other groups, which included several nuns and many international students. One day my friend and I were walking to the main bus station together. On the way was a large piece of land, the site of the old bus station, where big sheds still stood. We never went under them, they looked so creepy; nevertheless, it was a common walk for students. That day I noticed a van parked under the sheds. We were slightly ahead of the rest of our group and busy chatting as we passed the driver. I thought he was having a smoke, but then I was appalled to see his trousers were open. "Hey, Ginge," he said, "grab this!" I clutched my friend and together we ran so fast we were gasping for breath by the time we reached the station.

We talked about reporting it to the college the next day, but we were too scared. Other classmates, we found, had seen the same thing and hadn't told anyone. A day or so later I plucked up the courage to tell Mum at lunchtime. After lunch when I reached the college, I found a detective and a policewoman waiting in the entrance for me. The principal didn't look too happy. They hadn't told him what it was about, saying only that they wanted to discuss a case and needed to interview me.

They asked me to name the part of his body the flasher had exposed. My face went so red I thought I was going to catch fire. I just wanted to cry. To my relief, an officer suggested we say the man was exposing his person. If he came back, the police advised, we should call them immediately.

How could Mum have done this to me? This was the first time I had asked her advice, and she had called the police without warning me. I would never tell her anything again. I went home fuming. Eventually I told Mum and Dad the questions the police had asked me, and they started laughing. Dad said I should have told them it was Percy I saw. I had to laugh, but I wanted to cry more. Here I was, learning anatomy and physiology, yet I was too shy to say the organ was a penis. I was ashamed and embarrassed.

The man was seen many times, but the police were never quick enough to catch him. Oh, why did this have to happen to me? It was the last thing I'd expected to deal with in school, especially after what had happened to me in the past.

• • •

As time went by, I couldn't believe the changes at home. Dad was on his very best behaviour. I began to wonder if it had all been a bad dream. Regardless, I would not let down my guard. Mum was still happy telling her neighbours what to do, always wearing the pants, as Dad would say. Babs was three and a half and getting cuter by the day. Her golden hair was so pretty and her face was covered in freckles.

At college I met several engineers, including one from Canada who told us all about his family in Nova Scotia. Then there was Glenn from Saudi Arabia. He looked Arabic and often smoked a pipe, like my grand-dad. It was amazing to talk to people from the other side of the world.

Glenn took me to the pictures a couple of times. When he came to our house to pick me up, my parents were nice to him, but later they told me he might have some black colour in his background. I was beginning to think this discrimination was wrong. No matter what his background, he was a very nice person and was doing very well in his career. I had no reason to run to the other side of the street, as I had when I was young. Like all the engineers, he had to go back to sea and was away for months on the coastal vessels. By the time he came back, I was seeing someone else.

John was a twenty-three-year-old engineer with reddish-blonde hair. He was from Scunthorpe, across the water in Lincolnshire. We spent all our breaks chatting, and every weekend he asked me to walk with him to the ferry when he went home. On his last week we went to the pictures and he held me very close and kissed me. I walked him to the ferry for the last time. Again we kissed, and he held me so tight. As we said goodbye, I knew he could be the love of my life. However, time went by and I heard nothing. I was very hurt. "No more engineers for me," I told myself.

Joyce had new boyfriend, Laurie, a navigator in the Royal Air Force. After he was introduced to her by a friend of her mum's, he asked her where she worked. The next morning when Boots (the drugstore where she worked) opened, he went in and asked her to go out with him. It was love at first sight. They have been together ever since, sixty-one years now.

Meanwhile I focused on my work. I was doing well and getting good marks. We spent two weeks touring the city hospitals, and it was quite an eye-opener. The large infirmary, despite its excellent reputation, did not impress me at all. The first thing we were told was that student nurses were not allowed into the nurses' sitting room for the first ten weeks.

I was chagrined. It sounded like the upper class telling you that you weren't good enough. In England class distinctions still carried weight. If you had an accent, you were common, unrefined. You had to speak posh, as they called it, or you wouldn't fit in. In my mind everyone was equal. If you worked extra hard and did well, you deserved a pat on the back no matter where you lived. This kind of thing put me totally off the infirmary.

I liked the mental hospital, where our instructor worked, and I found the TB unit very interesting. They must have saved the best for last, though. I walked into Kingston General Hospital on Beverley Road and knew immediately it was where I wanted to be. The street leading up to it was full of houses owned by the hospital — the nurses' residences. None of them opened onto the main street; you had to enter through the hospital gate and sign in and out. The lounge and dining room had cozy, comfy couches. The curtains were cream, with pretty pink flowers matching the couches. I knew I could feel at home there.

Ben

We were at the tuck shop discussing which hospitals we liked, when suddenly my friend Rachael pointed out a young man who had approached us a week or so earlier. She wanted to know what I thought about him. He was smartly dressed in a grey suit with a nice blue shirt and seemed pleasant enough. I had the feeling he was kind to his mother. But what did it matter anyway? I wasn't going to speak to him. He kept on smiling at me, so I smiled back out of politeness.

The next morning I realized we were walking side by side up the main staircase. Then, going home, I noticed him wheeling a racing cycle; he had stopped to put on ankle clips. The following morning on the staircase, there he was again. He stepped aside to let me go up first, and when we reached the top he paused and asked me if I was in the nursing course. He told me he was a marine engineer studying to sit for his First Class Steam Certificate. His name was Ben.

From that point on, we seemed to talk more in the tuck shop. Then he began walking with me to the bus station on days when he didn't ride his bicycle to school. He used to belong to a cycling club that had been to Switzerland, where he won a silver medal, but during his seven-year marine engineer apprenticeship he hadn't been able to cycle very often. He asked me to the cinema the following weekend and we enjoyed each other's company.

Soon after, Mum and Dad decided to take Barbara to Primrose Valley in Filey and asked me to go with them. They had booked a caravan. Ben wanted to cycle down for a day, but I was a bit hesitant as he hadn't yet met my parents. They said he was welcome to come.

We went down by train and were picked up at the top road by a little bus, which carried us and our luggage to the bottom of the valley. Our campsite was a mile down, in a lovely lane of trees and flowers. The camp had its own shops and a roller-skating rink, though I knew I wouldn't be allowed to skate because it wasn't ladylike. The sands were warm and the sea was blue and sparkling in the sun.

When Ben arrived Mum fussed around getting him tea after his long ride. We had a nice lunch and then headed to the beach. Barbara loved making sandcastles and we all paddled in the sea. I noticed that every time Ben and I started to walk off, Mum was right behind us and would give Barbara to me. It was obvious she didn't want us to be on our own. Dad enjoyed talking to Ben; they had a lot in common regarding engineering.

When the time came for Ben to go, I said I would walk to the end of the valley to see him off. Straight away, Mum told me to take Babs with me. I said, "It's too far for her to walk." Also, Ben and I hadn't had a chance to have a conversation on our own. I said I would walk the mile to the top and come back on the bus. Mum didn't like that, by the look on her face. It was lovely to walk through the valley. We had a nice chat and kissed goodbye. I really liked him and looked forward to seeing him again.

After Ben and I had been going out for about six weeks, he showed me a small box containing a pretty white dogwood brooch. I said his mum would love it. "It's not for my mum," he said. "It's for you."

I told him there was no way I could accept it. Mum would not approve. He explained how surprised he'd been that I hadn't asked him for one thing since we had met. It was common for the engineers to go dancing, usually with Irish nurses, and he said the nurses seemed to expect the engineers to buy them drinks and cigarettes. Because I'd never asked him for anything, he wanted to buy me a present. I told him I still couldn't accept it. Maybe when I had known him much longer, my mum and dad might approve. I also pointed out that I wouldn't be able to go dancing or drinking. I wasn't old enough to do the latter. He said it didn't bother him at all, and for now he would put the brooch away for me.

He took me to meet his mum and his older brother Frank, who lived at home. Their older brother, Joe, was away in the Army. His mum was a tiny grey-haired lady, and we got on very well from the start. Like his mum, Ben wasn't tall, though his brothers were taller and heavier.

The more Mum and Dad saw Ben, the more they liked him. He and Dad were always talking about engines or the sea, and Dad borrowed Ben's engineering books to read. Mum was all fussy, telling everyone that if she had to pick a husband for me, he would be the one.

At twenty-three, Ben was six and a half years older than me. I did wonder if he would get a little bored with me, as he had liked to have a drink and go dancing, but it hadn't seemed to bother him so far. We spent most of our time studying at his house. During breaks, we would have a cup of tea with his mum. Sometimes we watched the TV, something I had never done before, as no one in our family had one. It was black and white with four stations. I especially loved the war movies and the musicals.

Next year I would be moving into a hospital, and happily I was accepted at my choice, Kingston General. Ben was going back to sea, probably for six months this time. His mum asked if I would come over to see her every week while he was away. Frank was a long-distance driver, so she would enjoy the company.

Before he left, out of nowhere Ben asked me if I would marry him if we felt the same towards each other when he came back. I told him I wouldn't go out with anyone else while he was away. I felt he was the one I would be happy to share my life with.

• • •

At the end of the year I sat the government nursing exam, Part 1 of the Nursing Registration. The results would take a while to come back. In the meantime I was called to have my measurements taken for my uniform. The student nurses wore lilac dresses with white butterfly hats. The dresses had to be a certain length below the knee, and anyone who altered them would be dealt with by the Matron. We all learned quickly that nobody would enjoy a visit to her office.

The seamstress showed us the correct way to fold our hats, which had to be worn at all times. We were given starched aprons for everyday use. They were pinned to our chest and had to be flipped over at twelve o'clock exactly; then we would be clean for the rest of the day. Long hair had to be tied back, and if it was short it could not touch the collar. We were reminded before we left — dress, hat, apron and hair. Should we disobey, we would visit the Matron.

We bought our own black shoes, which had to have a small heel to avoid flat arches. We also bought our own black stockings, and most of us chose fifteen denier, which was considered sexier than thick lisle. We were given a black cloak to wear when walking around the hospital. It was very warm and had a bright red lining and straps across the chest.

If you were under eighteen, you had to live in the nurses' homes. This would be the first time I earned a regular wage and would be able to pay for my room and board. Most of my friends had started work at fifteen; they went to dances and bought their own clothes. Now I would be able to do the same thing. Throughout college I had the same pocket money, two and sixpence, along with Aunty Ivy's shilling, which was a godsend – three and sixpence in all.

Dad had tried to get me a government grant, but his naval pension brought him ten shillings over the level required. I was quite upset to find several girls in my class had received the grant and it was six times the amount I had to manage on. However, I knew that if I was going to do what I had set out to do, I would manage somehow. I used Pond's reasonably priced makeup, and as long as my hair was neat, I felt happy. I brushed my hair one hundred times a night to make it shine and always rinsed it in vinegar after washing. If I had a piece of hair out of place, I would get the scissors and chop it off.

Mum and Dad said that after eighteen I would be able to move back home. My wage contribution would then help them buy Barbara's shoes and clothes, which I thought quite fair. Ben and I did a lot of serious talking about the future. Ben would be away and I was starting a new career, so we would have to see what the next few months held for us.

I was informed that my uniform was ready, so I could move into the hospital. Before I left home, a government letter came for me. I held my breath as I opened it. I had passed my exam. I cried with relief when I saw my results. It had all been worth it.

Life in the Hospital

We were escorted to our houses as new student nurses. The sitting rooms were downstairs, and upstairs were the large bedrooms. You could actually walk through four houses at a time, because they were all connected.

I loved the room I was given, with its big window and its modern furniture — a single bed with a side table, a wardrobe, and a dressing table with lots of drawers and a big mirror. Two of my friends were to share the room next door. Down the hall was a huge bathroom with lots of sinks and showers. We couldn't wish for a better accommodation. I only had one worry — my shyness to undress in front of anyone else. But that was easily solved. I would get up at least half an hour before we were called at six o'clock.

Mum had scared me with her nursing stories. She said when they went for injections or medical examinations, they were all lined up naked, as in the Army. The Sister walked through the line and checked for body hair. If any was found, they were told to get rid of that filth. From that day on, Mum had always shaved her private parts. Now it was my turn for a medical. I kept praying the same thing wouldn't happen to us. I couldn't thank Him enough when it didn't. Times had changed.

Betty went to another hospital, but there were six of us left from college. For the first three months, the student nurses with their Part 1 would attend school in the mornings and then in the afternoons and evenings work in the Syringe Department, Diet Kitchen, Outpatients Department or on the wards.

On our first working day we were called at six o'clock in the morning, sent to breakfast, and told our assignments at seven sharp. I got up at five o'clock and met Rachael, but we were too excited to eat breakfast. This was our first mistake. Our morning break would not be till ten thirty, and by then we were starving. By two o'clock we were ready for our lunch break. Our working day was from seven in the morning to eight at night, with a two-hour break around mid-afternoon. We had one day off a week and, if the hospital wasn't busy, one evening off also, though this didn't happen often. Most of us spent our breaks with our feet up in the sitting room. We chatted, studied and became friends.

Four of us had been assigned to the Syringe Department. Back then every syringe and needle used was dealt with separately. Our job was to make sure each went through the four trays of strong disinfectant, which sometimes burnt our hands. We would lay them in the first tray and squirt in the disinfectant, then examine the needles to make sure they weren't bent and the ends were sharp. The practical nurse in charge was elderly, strict, and very mean at times. When one girl spoke out, saying she thought what she had done was correct, the nurse told her she wasn't paid to think. I disagreed. In nursing you had to think about everything you did very carefully, for the safety of your patients.

Before I left for college Mum had given me orders to stop in at home every evening, but with all the new adjustments I didn't go home until the fourth night. I came off duty at eight o'clock, rushed to my room to grab my raincoat, and ran up the street to catch a bus to town. As I opened the door Mum called out, "Where do you think you've been? It's four days since you left here."

I explained that the trip had taken me an hour and fifteen minutes, running most of the way. There was no way I could have got home and back in two hours, even if I'd missed lunch. I hadn't eaten yet tonight, but I could only stay for a quick cup of tea because I had to check in at the nurses' house by eleven. Mum made me a sandwich and I promised to come home on my day off. As I was signing in at the hospital gate, two Sisters were already on their way to lock us in. I knew I would not be going out at night unless I was lucky enough to get a free evening.

At school our instructor was another elderly lady, a spinster whose family had been with the hospital for many years. Strict she was, but extremely kind. Her first demand was that we never say the word *sweat*; we must say *perspire*. Our college instructor had warned us that some hospital Sisters were fussy about the word, though he said *sweat* was normal. The rest of the lecture was about caring for our patients and treating them with dignity and respect. There was no doubt in my mind that all these people were there only to care for the patients.

I realized we hadn't even thought about our salaries or the long hours. Most of us were born during the war, so everyone was used to people taking care of each other. To us it was a natural thing to do, and we just wanted to do a good job. Nevertheless, we were excited to see our first real pay packet. At the end of the month we were given a tiny yellow envelope. The slip inside stated our hours of work, which was usually sixty or more per week, tax deductions towards the English Pension, and the cost of room and board. I was surprised to see how much we paid for board and lodging, but they did provide our uniforms and do our laundry. Our food was good and plentiful, our rooms were spotless, and our surroundings were nice and comfortable.

Our total earnings were just over nine pounds. What was left in the envelope was a one pound note, a ten shilling note and a few coins. I actually had money to pay for my bus fares home and my black stockings. Wearing a uniform all the time, I didn't have to buy many clothes, so maybe I would even be able to save a tiny bit. It was terrific, considering what I had managed on before.

• • •

I made a new friend named Margaret, and after a while we became quite close and began to confide in each other. Never about Dad – there was only Joyce who knew about that. Joyce was still working for Boots downtown. Now and again I popped in and made a date to go to her house. Ann worked in a bakery shop, and I stopped in to see her occasionally when I went to Grandma's. If she wasn't in, I would go in and see her mum and dad. In fact, I saw a number of our old neighbours. They were always around, still helping each other out.

Dad was on his usual shifts, so I didn't see much of him. When I did, I could see a difference in him. I realized he hadn't made any advances since I'd almost had a nervous breakdown. It was as if those things had never happened. I think my being ill had really scared him. I was so relieved.

Whenever Ben wanted to talk to me, he had to call from a public phone and leave a message at the nurses' house saying what time he might call. One day he called and told me he would be leaving soon to join his ship for six months. Half a year. I knew the next six months would be busy for me, but nothing would be the same without him. I would miss him very much. I promised to visit his mum and Frank weekly as I had before, which pleased him.

My days off started early, at home with Babs. Then I would go to Grandma's to see Uncle Ted, who was now very fragile. Aunty Ivy usually came home before I left. I also tried to visit Ben's mum. If I couldn't do it all in one day, I would go see Ben's mum when I had an evening off, which usually started at six. Occasionally Frank dropped me off on his motorbike, which was quicker than the bus. It was certainly a busy life.

I also had to keep my letters going. I received quite a few from Ben, who often sent comical postcards about love, usually with cute puppies. It was a little embarrassing, because our nurse in charge delivered our mail. Before putting them in our slots, she would read everything she could, checking who and where they came from and commenting on everything written on the postcards.

One day Rachael asked if I would like to go to a dance at City Hall. It sounded exciting; I had never been allowed to go to a dance before. Then I remembered my promise to Ben, so I didn't go. The day after the dance, Rachael had come home late; her pass had only been for midnight. Lucky for her, someone pulled her in through a window.

She had a message to pass on to me. My heart jumped when she told me it was from a friend of John's." He told her he would like to explain why John didn't get in touch with me again, so she could pass it on to me. When John met me in college, he had fallen head over heels in love with me. What John hadn't told me was that he had been engaged to a girl in Scunthorpe for a long time. They went to school together and both families were friends, always expecting them to marry.

When he met me, he went home intending to break off the engagement. Then he began to think that since he was older than me, I might not want to become serious. Then nervous about the effect it would have on the families, he decided to leave things as they were.

As Rachael told me this, tears rolled down my cheeks. I knew John had really been my first love. I just wished with all my heart he could have talked to me. Then he would have known exactly how I felt about him. Age didn't matter to me. Ben was the same age as John.

I wished now I had gone to the dance with Rachael and talked to his friend myself. However, Rachael told him I was serious with Ben so I'm sure he would pass it on to John. It was good she had gone that night; it was such a relief to know the reason after all this time. Like many things in our lifetime, it maybe was not meant to be.

• • •

After three months in the Syringe Department, we were all sent to the Special Diet Kitchen. It was unbelievable how many different diets we had to learn about. Every day we baked twenty-three salt-free loaves for heart patients and helped clean twenty-three chickens. It was the same way Gran cleaned them, only we wore gloves to pull out the intestines.

My next assigned department was Outpatients. The Heart Clinic was led by a South Asian doctor who did most of the surgery. Not only was he in charge of his clinic but he was continually checking the nurses to make sure they did things properly. A nurse would prepare the patients for him and, if the patient was female, lift her breast for him to listen to her heart.

The student nurses used to observe while he examined his patients. We had to be alert because he often asked us questions. He always wanted to test us, even if we were new. Some student nurses tried to hide in the sterilization room, but I found I learned a lot from his method. It forced one to think.

One day after examining a patient he told me to look closely at the man's chest and tell him what I saw. I felt my face go red, and he told me to take my time. I took a deep breath. Observation, we were told, was most important. After staring at the patient's chest, I said I thought his skin was a bit yellowish and his chest was higher on one side than the other. I nearly fell over when the doctor said I was quite correct. Then he asked which side was higher and what might be the cause. It was definitely the left side, so I pointed to that. All I could think of was that the heart was on the left side and if it was enlarged it might be pushing his chest up. It was a quick answer, and I prayed he wouldn't ask me any more questions. He said, "Correct again. Excellent." He gave his patient some instructions and then walked straight out of the room.

Besides the Heart Clinic, this doctor had another clinic for various problems, often hemorrhoids. He always made the patient, young or old, strip naked. If they were old, it never seemed to worry me. When it was young men, I saw by their red faces how embarrassed they were. Our teaching dictated that a nurse should never show her personal feelings or make comments that would embarrass patients, even if she had to listen to foul language. We were told it might be part of the patient's background or they might not know any better. We were not here to judge. Again, respect and dignity were what we were taught, how to understand why people reacted in certain ways. In this case, I decided that instead of staring at red faces and full frontal views of patients' private parts, I would take a step back the minute the doctor turned them around. It seemed to put the patients at ease. I wasn't sure the doctor would like me moving back and forth, but he never said a word.

One day when I was moving the patients through to the examination area, the doctor came out of the room yelling at the nurse. He went to

Sister and said, "Give this nurse something else to do and give me the sensible one." He came over to me and grabbed my arm, pulling me into the room. I guess I should have felt honoured. Instead I only felt bad for the other girl.I was transferred to the Male Surgical Ward. I would be under the guidance of two graduate nurses, nurses who had passed their SRN (state registered nurse) exams but were waiting to receive their certificates. When the Sister introduced me to them, I had to quickly pull myself together. The two nurses were from Nigeria. In the weeks that followed, I came to realize they were the most helpful people I could ever have met. Again, this made me think about what I had been taught as a child. There was something very wrong there for sure. I laughed when I thought of eccentric Catholics. Ben was Catholic, so now I was dating one.

I worked on two surgical wards with at least twenty patients in each. The wards were extremely long, so we had to almost gallop along to get to the end. We were allowed to walk quickly but never to run. Only in an emergency, a fire, or a hemorrhage were we allowed to do that. Years later I still get told to slow down.

Our first job on the ward was to get a bucket of hot water and some disinfectant to wipe the bed frames before the beds were made up. We emptied all the urinals and bedpans and sterilized them. Then we made all the beds with envelope corners and set up all the trolleys for different procedures. As newer nurses came in, they took over the frame-washing and bedpans. The newer you were, the dirtier the jobs you were assigned.

Before surgery it was routine to give patients enemas and then shave the area being operated on. The enemas seemed to become my regular job. It was quite a chore, and it was a little tricky learning not to cut anyone with the razors. Inevitably as I pushed the trolley through the wards someone would call out, "Here comes the enema queen!"

I always felt more at ease with the male patients. They were easygoing and rarely complained. I had always heard that if men were sick at home they acted like babies. Perhaps one or two in the hospital were like this, but not many, in my estimation. Women, I worried about, because I thought they might boss me around like my mum. I came to understand that if they were a bit grumpy it was usually because they wanted to get home quickly to look after their families. They were used to running everything at home while their husbands provided the income, and being sick was a nuisance and irritation for them.

Two of our patients died a week after their surgeries. A male nurse came and asked me to help him lay one of them out. I was told to wait near the bed till the nurse came back with the trolley. The body was covered, and I wondered what it was going to look like. When the patient had been alive he hadn't looked good, with all the tubes down his throat and needles in his arms.

I stood still, with both arms behind my back. We didn't have curtains around the bed, just screens. The sun shining through the window seemed to bounce tiny rays off the white bedspread. It looked as if the bedspread was moving. I started sweating and felt myself begin to panic. The nurse had been gone so long, I wondered if he was coming back.

Finally the nurse returned, and he pulled off the cover. It was a terrible sight, yellow bile running out of the patient's mouth where the tubes had been and blood and fluid leaking from the needles in his arms. Below, where his bowel surgery had been done, the sheets were covered in blood and feces.

I was told we had to pull him up by his arms into a sitting position and remove his gown. As we did this, there was a loud blast of gas from his mouth that sounded like a groan. I began to shake and my teeth chattered. "We're not supposed to laugh," said the nurse.

"I am definitely not going to laugh," I said. I was trying to stop myself from screaming or crying. I understood why other nurses were hysterical on occasion.

That wasn't the end. After we had thoroughly cleaned the body, I was asked to pass the nurse a long instrument off the trolley. This instrument was to pack bandages into the lower part of the body — the anus for males, the vagina for females. Then we dressed the body in a nice white shroud; we never have to do that sort of thing today. If a family wished to see the deceased, we would place the body in a small chapel before the funeral home came and took it away.

I had seen some horrible sights, going back to the babies in the burns ward I'd seen at age twelve. Colostomy surgery wasn't too pretty, either — I had several patients in a row who had their bowels outside their bodies for a few days, covered with gauze soaked in gel. Things have changed so much since then. Strangely no matter what I saw, the thing that frightened me was simply watching the end of a needle coming out of flesh.

My next ward was Women's Gynecology. As the newest on the ward, I got the dirtiest jobs. There were lots of bloody sheets, so we kept a bath full of cold water to soak them in before they went to the laundry. I had to examine each bedpan thoroughly before I emptied and sterilized it. We used to take them to what we called the "slough room." There were so many miscarriages in progress that if we found anything it had to be labelled and the RN notified at once. Once certain parts had been passed, the patient's chart was updated to document the stages of the miscarriage.

The first bedpan I took to the slough room had something in it that reminded me of when Mum had lost her baby. That I had never forgotten. I told the RN, and when I got back from my break, she had a message for me from the ward Sister. The note said I had made an excellent observation, something they hadn't expected from me on my first day on the ward. During my time there I found learning about women's problems very interesting.

After a few weeks I went on to the Women's Medical Ward. One of the patients there was a young woman, recently married, who had needed regular blood transfusions over the past several years. I was told she had a type of anemia and only had a very short time to live. It was so sad. Her young husband rarely left her side.

After I had been on the ward two weeks, another patient arrived. The minute she recognized me, her arms went around me. It was a kindly old teacher of mine from years ago, who had a serious heart condition. There I was, several days later, washing my teacher's back in the bath. Neither of us was embarrassed, and we chatted as if we were close friends. I was happy to be able to take care of her. It was sad when the time came for her to leave, for I knew this would be the last time I would see her. We hugged each other tightly and the tears rolled down my face.

Engaged

Ben's six months at sea finally came to an end. I couldn't wait to see him. He sent me a message to meet at the bus station as usual, and when I stepped off the bus he was right there. It seemed strange after all this time to see someone I loved waiting for me. I thought of how it must have been for Mum and Dad when he was abroad fifteen years out of twenty-two.

There was so much to say. We decided to go back to his mum's, as it was nearer. His mum was very happy to see him, but she gave us some time alone to talk, something that didn't happen very often in our house. Ben was home for two or three weeks, and then he would be joining a new ship. This time he would be away for five days at a time. His ship would run between Bremen and Denmark and then back to Immingham, which was just across the water in Lincolnshire.

A few days later Ben's brother Joe came home, and Ben suggested we should get engaged while he was here. I worried about what my parents would say. I knew Dad would say yes, but Mum, I dared not guess. Ben wanted to ask Dad first, the correct thing to do, but I thought if Mum was told first she would feel in charge and that might make a difference. So I told her Ben had asked me to get engaged and asked what she thought about it. She was all smiles and said, "Next time he comes over, ask him to ask your Dad."

On my next day off we went to see them together. Before we were through the door, we knew by their smiles that permission would be granted. While Mum was making tea in the kitchen, Ben asked Dad and got his approval. Mum suggested that, as it was my eighteenth birthday the next weekend, we could invite Ben's family over for a small celebration.

I asked Ben not to overdo it on the ring where money was concerned. We went downtown and Ben checked a very popular jewellery shop window. There was so much to look at, I didn't know what I wanted. Then I saw a pretty slope ring with three diamonds set in gold and platinum, and we both liked it. The only other jewellery I'd had was a ring from Aunty Ivy when I was little and a fob watch on my uniform, so this was really special. Ben had talked me into accepting the dogwood brooch just before he went away. A relative said how pretty it was on my coat, and when I told her my boyfriend had bought it for me she said, "They only buy you things like that because they want sex in return." Why do people always seem to look on the bad side of things? Mum thought the ring was too expensive, but gorgeous.

We had our celebration two days before my eighteenth birthday. Joe brought his and Ben's mum, though sad to say Frank didn't come. I baked sausage rolls and Mum cooked a lovely dinner. There was a big cake that was both a birthday cake and an engagement cake together. After the party, as Joe and his mum were about to leave, Mum said, "Hope you enjoyed this. Thank you for coming. There will be no more celebrations until Pat is twenty-one." The message was loud and clear. Joe looked as if he was going to make a comment but changed his mind at the last minute. His mum smiled, thanked Mum for the dinner and told me they had loved my sausage rolls.

On my actual birthday Ben gave me another gift, a gold Swiss watch. I was overwhelmed. Dad's gift was money, and Mum suggested I use it for a down payment on a new bike. Now that I was eighteen, she reminded me, I could live at home again. I would see more of Barbara, who I really missed. Getting to and from work would lengthen my day, as I would have to get up at a quarter to five. I thought of my nice student room and independence. But now that I had been away, they surely would treat me more like an adult.

I decided to come home, only to find that Mum had all her rules ready. I had to be in the house by eleven o'clock. The problem was that films finished at exactly ten thirty. If I could catch the last bus from the theatre, I would be dead on time, but if I had to take the next one, I would be five minutes late. Whenever that happened, I would find Mum behind the door and Dad behind her, shouting, "Where have you been?" Oh dear!

• • •

The more Ben and I saw each other during his breaks, the more we wanted to be together and settle down. We wanted to get married and have a nice flat of our own away from my parents' supervision and their ever-watching eyes. They wouldn't even let us go to my room to study together. There was a National Union of Seamen downtown, which had food, drink and lodging at very reasonable rates. Ben had it in mind that if we got married, we could go to the London Union to spend a few days there for our honeymoon. I told him not to get his hopes up.

Occasionally we went downtown to buy my black stockings at a shop near the Union. Often we would bump into his fellow engineers. We chatted with one in particular who went steady for two years with a very nice girl but never managed to coax her into having sex. They finally married and had a child and seemed very happy, but not long after, he told Ben he had been intimate with another woman. I knew these things happened, but having seen his wife and how beautiful she was, I couldn't believe it. What was wrong with this man? I asked Ben if it was common for seamen to do this, thinking of my dad also. Was it because they were away for so long?

A few months later we saw this chap again, looking very pale and tired. I left them to their usual chat. This time Ben told me his friend had just left the doctor's office, where he had been told he had VD (venereal disease). He was worried about what excuse he could give his wife to avoid having sex. I was totally disgusted.

Just the week before, I had discovered a special ward I hadn't known existed. Our ward Sister had asked me to go to an unfamiliar building, which I had assumed was where the war veterans had an extended care ward. Sister said it was near there, but it was very private. It was a ward only for people with syphilis and gonorrhea. I was told these types of diseases were incurable after a certain stage without treatment.

The ward was hard to find and there were only five people in it. There were no older people, as I had expected. It looked like a sitting room, and patients wore their normal clothes. This was their home. I chatted with them a few minutes and then left the file I had brought for the RN. I couldn't get it into my head that they were going to die there.

My dad came to mind, away all those years. I decided I couldn't go there in my thoughts. I could never talk about those matters freely with anyone, apart from Joyce. It was well over thirty years later, when I took a counselling course, that I first discussed them with anyone else.

• • •

One day as I was sitting with my friend Margaret, I sensed she was worried about something. Her boyfriend was away like mine, but before he left they had discussed the subject of sex. In those days sex before marriage was strongly frowned upon. Margaret was afraid something was wrong with her — that she might be deformed — and that her boyfriend might not want to marry her because of it.

Oh my, that word *deformed!* A word I had first heard my mother use to me when I was ten. One night as I lifted my nightdress to go potty, she said my private parts were deformed. I told Margaret we both might have the same problem. Margaret couldn't believe it. She suggested writing to a doctor's column in a magazine. We made up a letter together, hoping he would answer us. If there was something really wrong, we didn't know how we were going to tell our boyfriends. It was a relief to know there was somebody else in the same boat.

Ten weeks later we had almost given up when Margaret finally received an answer from the doctor. It was good news. The doctor explained that everyone was different and that what we were worrying about was totally normal. Of course, we had worried for so many years, it wasn't likely to go away immediately, but we were glad we wouldn't have to explain it to our boyfriends before we married. I have to admit that until I had my first child, it was still on my mind.

Changing Course

During one of Ben's visits to our house, he turned straight to Dad and asked how he felt about us getting married soon. Mum had gone upstairs for something and Babs was asleep. To my surprise, Dad smiled and said he was very happy about it. I held my breath when I heard Mum come back downstairs. I knew this wasn't going to end well.

"No way," she said angrily. "That's not going to happen until she's twenty-one. Forget it. When she gets married, she's going to have her own house."

"I don't think they need a house. They'd be happy if they lived in a tent together," said Dad.

Ben pleaded with her. "Pat has been a responsible person in her job. If we have a flat to begin with, we can save to buy our own house. There's no reason she can't continue with her nursing." No matter what he said, Mum wouldn't agree.

"Mum," I said, "who in our family has ever owned their own home?"

"Well, you're going to be different." After that she simply said no to everything. By the end, she was yelling and screaming at all of us. She declared that Ben was not welcome in our house ever again.

I walked Ben to the bus and left Mum and Dad arguing. When I returned I went straight to bed. The next morning I didn't take Mum her cup of tea and left as fast as I could. That night when I came home it was just Dad and Babs. I put Babs to bed and went down to talk to Dad. He told me Mum had packed her bags and left. Dad was on day shifts, so there was no one to take care of Babs, only me. Mum had done this once before, after she'd had a tiff with Dad. Now she'd left a toddler behind. I had no choice but to call in sick.

She had done this deliberately to punish both Dad and me. We heard three days later that Mum was staying with a friend of Aunty Ivy. On the fifth day she turned up again, still demanding that Dad agree with what she wanted or else she wasn't coming home. I had lost five days' work – this couldn't go on. In the end Dad said he had no choice but to agree with her. Mum's absence wasn't good for Barbara, and if it went on any longer it might ruin my job. Above all, he had to live there and keep the peace. He said he liked Ben very much and wished he could just say yes. I totally understood, because we all knew it was Mum who always had and always would wear the pants in our house. I told him not to worry, Ben and I would sort it all out.

Mum came home. The next morning I brought her tea at five o'clock as usual. The moment she was awake she began to shout and curse about Ben and call him every name she could possibly think of. I guess this was the only time of day she would see me, so she had to get it off her chest. This went on for months. She was determined to break us up if it was the last thing she did. I didn't dare risk Ben coming to the gate, in case she decided to throw something at him. The only place we could meet was at the bus station.

At work I began to shake every time I picked up my knife and fork. I couldn't stop hiccupping when I ate, and I began to feel a lot of pain in my stomach. What a wreck I was. Other people began to notice. One or two nurses offered me cigarettes, thinking smoking might calm me and stop my shaking. Mum had always said if I ever smoked she would put the lighted end down my throat, but at this point I didn't care. I was feeling like a rebel. I knew most people had a hard time giving it up once they started — both Mum and Aunty Ivy had smoked for years before they quit — but when I tried it, I soon found the smoke went up my nose and into my eyes, which began to water, and then I started coughing. It was for the best, as I knew I couldn't afford it. From then on I never had the urge to continue.

I hated going home, but if I went back to live at the nurses' house, I was sure Mum would turn up somehow. She wouldn't think twice of what it would do to my job and my training. Nothing would stop her getting her own way.

The pain in my stomach increased, and Mum started threatening to go to the hospital and talk to the Matron. I didn't want anybody to know my business. Our system was very strict, but as long as I did a good job my own life was private. I told Ben that if Mum did this, it would be the end of me. I honestly couldn't face the embarrassment. I said maybe we should break things off for a while. If we waited till I was twenty-one, I wouldn't need anyone's permission.

Ben's face went white. "When you have your holidays," he said, "we could go to Gretna Green and get married." Gretna Green is in Scotland; there you could get married when you were sixteen.

The next time I went to meet Ben on my day off, his bus arrived but there was no sign of him. The buses ran every half hour. When two had come and gone, I thought I had better go to his house. Unless his ship had left early – and without phones he couldn't let me know – I didn't know what to think.

When I arrived at his house, Frank came to the door. "Thank God you're here," he said. "I just got home to find Ben in a terrible state. His eyes are red from crying and he's flat-out drunk. He's been drinking rum. Goodness knows how much." I explained everything to Frank over a cup of tea and ended up crying. We talked for a long time. Frank said he'd never seen Ben in such a state. Finally Ben woke up and said he couldn't think of us splitting up even for a little while. I told him not to worry anymore, that no matter what, we would stick together. It seemed the more we had to face, the stronger our bond became.

I went to see my doctor about the stomach pain and the shaking. The first thing he asked was "Are you having any stress at home?" He remembered the time I hadn't been able to stop crying for three days and had been very near a breakdown. I sat with him for a while and told him what had been going on. He had known my family for years. While Mum was a good person, he said, she tended to dominate a little too much, especially with her family. He told me I had to have some tests done and we would have another good talk when he got the results. I felt much better just being able to discuss things with him.

I returned to see him the following week. He shook his head when he read my papers. The results were not good. I had a peptic ulcer, which might take a long time to heal. I was also very anemic. He said the best advice he could give me was to leave home as soon as I could. He also said to change my job because it was too stressful. Otherwise, within three months I would have a total nervous breakdown.

But I was tough. Surely I would get over this. I went home and told Mum I had been to the doctor and discovered I had a peptic ulcer and anemia. She then laughed in my face. "Poor dear," she said sarcastically. "You'll have a few more ulcers after I've been to your Matron's office." I knew then that I somehow had to put a stop to all this. What was I going to do?

Margaret told me I was welcome to stay with her family. She said her mum could do with the board and lodging money. It was a nice offer, but there were seven people there already. I couldn't ask my grandma because she was busy looking after Uncle Ted. Also, she was sure to agree with Mum. Aunty Ivy wouldn't take my side, especially after Iris. I could tell Dad didn't like what was going on, but he couldn't do anything about it. All Ben knew was that I was planning to move out, not that I'd begun thinking of giving notice and looking for another job.

I didn't know where to start. I felt as if I was going out of my head, giving up the only thing I'd ever wanted to do in my life. I made up my mind to go to Margaret's house. I had to pay a month's rent in advance, so I needed to find a new job soon.

I went to do the paperwork with the hospital secretary, and straight away she tried to convince me to stay. I thought about asking to move back in, but I knew what would happen if I did — Mum would go to the Matron and tell her I refused to go home. The secretary said they weren't allowed to show us our reports from the ward, but she showed me one anyway. It read "This student nurse has done extremely well. She has the makings of a perfect nurse in our profession." I thanked the secretary for her help, but I had made my mind up. I walked out of the hospital for the last time, my heart heavy with sadness. All I had worked for was gone. I was numb.

I was going to start a life without my parents and my sweet little sister. I would always worry about Barbara and miss her, but I refused to go on living in fear of what Mum would do. I didn't want all this stress. Mum would tell everyone I had given up nursing up to get married, and they would probably believe her. I was not going to run around telling them all my business. No doubt she would say it was Ben's fault, but he and his family were as surprised as everyone else when they found out. It was the last thing Ben had wanted me to do.

I went home, packed my bags, and walked out the door. I was still in a trance and as numb as ever. I can't remember if anyone was in the house at the time. I think I left a note. I hoped one day Mum would realize just what she had done.

The Last Straw

Margaret's family all made me feel at home, which I was very grateful for. And I was totally free to see Ben on weekends and evenings every time he came home. It felt really strange.

I applied for a job with a large dry cleaning company, Zerny's, which had twenty-eight shops in Yorkshire and several other counties. The general manager was very pleasant. He asked if I was likely to go back to nursing, but I told him no. I started the following week in a downtown shop, where I met some terrific people who I would be working with for the next few years. Mary, our manager, would be there for me throughout my life whenever I needed her. She passed away recently at the age of eighty-nine, but she will be in my heart forever.

My new job was easy to learn, the girls were very pleasant, and it was a happy atmosphere. Mary and I often went into the market for lunch, where the food was reasonable and delicious. Once a week we went for fish and chips at the big café where the fish covered the plate and alongside it were mushy peas and too many chips. It also came with bread and butter — all for one shilling and sixpence.

I swore to myself that after all the studying I had done, I would never read anything again, only my *Woman's Weekly* magazine, which I had been collecting since I was seventeen. It had all the knitting patterns and recipes that I would ever need.

When Ben was home we spent most of our time researching flats. He still wanted to go to Gretna Green, but I wanted to give my parents a little time to come around. I guess we could have lived together, but in those days it was frowned upon. It seemed silly to me that at eighteen you could legally drink and do several other things, yet to get married you needed to be twenty-one.

We planned to have a small wedding in the Catholic church. If we were married in my church, Ben wouldn't be able to take communion. I had been to his church a few times. His mum went regularly, but not his brothers. For me, apart from the Latin service, there was little difference between the churches. Ben's attitude was that no one could agree with any church 100 percent on its teachings. Though nothing prevented me from attending my church, I had made up my mind I would not take his faith away from him. As far as bringing up our children as Catholics, I was marrying one, so it didn't bother me in the least. If they turned out like their dad and his family, I would be quite happy.

Weeks later I was feeling more relaxed, but my stomach was still not too good. At least my hands were shaking much less. There had been no word from home, but then I hadn't left an address. Ben saw a flat advertised in a nice area at a good price, so we decided maybe it was time to get in touch with Mum and Dad. I wrote a short note asking them both to come to Margaret's house.

The next day, someone banged loudly on the door. Ben was away, which was probably for the best. I opened the door and there was Mum. Quickly she brushed past me into the house and said in a loud voice, "Don't tell me. You've got yourself into trouble. You're pregnant!"

I looked her straight in the eye and burst out laughing. "I'm so sorry to disappoint you," I said, "but I'm not, Mum."

I told her about the flat, but she already knew all our plans and also where I had been living. Margaret's mum, it seemed, had seen her on the bus and had told her everything. After ranting and raving for a while, Mum made me an offer. I would come home and they would give us written permission to marry, on one condition — we must never tell our neighbours anything about what had been going on in our family. As if that was likely! I learned later that, of course, she had fallen out with them as well. I agreed to go home and told her Ben would put a deposit on the flat when he returned. I hoped they would keep their promise.

• • •

At home, the same rules as before were in effect. Ben was not allowed in the house. When I told Barbara and Dad our wedding plans, Mum was quiet. I told Barbara she was to be our flower girl. I had already bought her a pale yellow organdy dress that would be perfect with her hair. Our wedding date was March 31, Easter Saturday. We needed my parents' permission immediately because the banns had to be read for three weeks.

I had saved fifty pounds since I'd started work. Ben had a good job, but I didn't take it for granted that he would be able to pay for everything. When I told Mum, it was clear by the frown on her face that she wasn't pleased we were ahead with everything. I had hoped she would be proud of what I had done. Mum said she would like to pay for the three-tier cake we had ordered, and I hoped it was a sign that she and Dad would come to the wedding.

The minute I mentioned it was going to be in Corpus Christi Catholic Church, Mum went wild again. She said she hated Ben and I should marry his brother, Frank, who'd said he thought the world of me. I thought the world of him too, and Ben's mum and Joe. They were going to be my in-laws and I couldn't wish for any better. But I was engaged to Ben. I had known him for nearly three years. Dad liked him, and so had Mum until we wanted to get married. Nothing was going to change how we felt about each other, ever.

In the end she finally scribbled a note of permission to marry, signed it, and then almost threw it at me. She said to let her know when it was all done and sorted, and the sooner I could leave the better. She hardly spoke to me after that. I had been planning to ask her to go with me and choose my dress. I had left it till last, hoping everything would work out between us. In the end I asked Mary from work to go with me instead.

I picked a dress with a lace body and sleeves, and net panels that stood out at the bottom, with a short veil. When I took it home, I laid it out on my bed and asked Mum and Dad if they would like to look at it. Mum said no. Dad came up to see it and said it was lovely, but he looked very sad. He put his arm around my shoulder and gave me a hug. At dinner Mum told me Dad would not be giving me away and that none of our family would be coming to the wedding. I couldn't imagine walking down the aisle without being on my dad's arm. Who on earth could I ask to give me away? What about little Babs? They couldn't do such a thing to my little sister! But I didn't want to cause Gran any trouble, and I knew Aunty Ivy wouldn't go against my mum's wishes.

"By the way," Mum added, "if you dare announce in the *Daily Mail* that you're getting married in a Catholic church, I'll send your dad to the church to punch Ben in the nose." Dad waited till Mum was out of the way, then told me he was very sorry about all this. He wanted me to know it was not his decision. No one could have convinced me it was.

I had lived with Mum many years more than Dad and knew her too well. She would never change.

I told Mary how hurt I was, and as usual she had a solution – her husband Bill would be happy to give me away. Margaret suggested that her little sister Tricia, who was the same size and age as Babs, fill in as flower girl. Though Mum repeatedly said no one from our family would be coming, I kept hoping they would at the last minute. I wanted them there on my special day, no matter what. Even if they didn't come, they might let Babs come.

On my last day at home, I had everything packed. Mum put my lunch on the table, a lovely thick stew. I couldn't think of anything I could do to change her mind, but I had to try one more time. I asked if they would come to the wedding, and the answer was again no. She added, "You do realize, of course, that this is the last meal you'll ever eat in this house. When you leave and go through that door, you will never, ever come back through it again. You make your bed and lie on it."

I almost choked, and tears began rolling down my cheeks. "Mum," I said, "I don't want it to be this way and neither does Ben. But if that's what you want, then there's nothing I can do about it."

I still loved them all, and I knew I would miss them. I hoped one day my little Babs would understand all this. I really didn't want to leave her, but it had to be. I was glad Dad was at work. I got up, put on my coat and picked up my bags. I walked through the door for the last time. I told myself while I waited for the bus that from this moment on I would stand on my own two feet. I would never ask anyone for anything again.

To love

To love and be loved is a wonderful thing,
When the man in your life makes your heart want to sing.
The joys and the sorrows, when both of you share
Seem so small when there's two of you always to care.
Life has its turmoils, but trust God above.
One day he will find you your real, own true love.

The Wedding

Growing up, most girls had what we called our "bottom drawer," where we saved trinkets for our weddings. We embroidered cushion covers, tablecloths and sideboard runners. When my time came, I left home and went straight to the new flat and spent the whole day hanging fresh curtains and finding a place for everything. Ben came to help and we did what we could to make it cozy before he left for his cousin's home for his stag night.

It was a splendid flat, with a big front room downstairs and a spacious kitchen at the back of the house. Upstairs was a big bedroom with the bathroom next door. The flat was furnished, which was a big savings for us. Ben was sleeping at his mum's, so Margaret stayed over before the wedding. The bed was so high, we had to pull each other up and in as we kept falling off the edge. I would need a small stool to climb up when I was on my own.

The day we had been waiting for came at last. I was up at six o'clock and left to go and get the cushions. I asked the bridesmaids if they would mind tidying up the room, hoping I would be back at 10, to make the sandwiches. I came back at 11 to find the girls just getting out of bed. I took a quick shower and went to the kitchen, still in my dressing gown, to make the sandwiches. The wedding cake had been picked up the night before. I had just got started when the van arrived with the flowers. Then Frank came in with the buttonholes and we carried them upstairs. "I thought you'd be almost ready by now," he said. "It won't be long before the cars arrive." The cars were to pick us up at one thirty for the service at two o'clock.

Off he went, while I went back to the sandwiches. A few minutes later the doorbell rang again and in came Mary, Bill and her sister Sue. They chased me out of the kitchen and took over. I put on my dress while the bridesmaids got ready and Margaret saw to her little sister Tricia. I couldn't find my makeup anywhere, so Margaret lent me hers. Then they told me they couldn't find Tricia's headdress.

I remembered a lot of shopping bags had gone in the dustbin, so I ended up in the backyard bent over the dustbin, sorting through bags in my wedding dress. Mary and Sue thought I was out of my mind. It wasn't in there, so we decided to put a small ring of flowers on Tricia's head instead. I put on my veil, hoping to make it secure with pins. Mary was banging on the door telling us the cars were here. As Bill was walking me downstairs, I realized I hadn't checked my sleeves. All the studs up my arm were unfastened. We had twenty minutes in the car, so I fastened them on the way. Then, for the first time, I finally relaxed.

Our guests were some of Ben's relatives and a few of my friends from the hospital. The service was much shorter than the regular Catholic one, since ours was classed as a mixed marriage. The priest asked for a coin from Ben, a silver half-crown, which was blessed and put in a tiny white leather purse. It was a symbol of wealth, blessed to stay with me all my life. Six decades later, the tiny purse is in good condition, but the coin is totally green mould.

After signing the register we went to the entrance, to find my old friend Ann standing next to Gran's neighbour, Mrs. G. I gave them both a hug, and then I greeted our old bus driver and his wife, friends of Mum's. I tried not to cry, but I was really touched. Mrs. G had known me since I was born. I knew she would tell Gran how I looked. We had announced our wedding in the paper, and though I didn't believe Dad would hurt Ben, I was still worried about Mum's threat. But there was no one at all from my family.

When our party of about twenty, including Ann, arrived at the flat, we found a big box on the doorstep, a beautiful crystal water set from Mrs. G. Ben was very happy and got a bit tipsy at our little party. All he could say after the vows was "We're together now. No one can ever take you away from me."

In the evening we got ready for our honeymoon trip to London. Joe and Frank took us to the railway station, after Joe got Ben to splash his face with water, as he was looking a little pale. It had been quite a while since he'd drunk so much. As he said, "I really have something to celebrate."

The train was full during our five-hour trip to London, and Ben slept all the way, but when we got there he was fine. Lucky for me, he carried the luggage. I had a whole new wardrobe — Ben had bought me two lovely under sets from Denmark, one pale blue and the other yellow, and

I had bought myself a lilac nightdress and another in pale yellow. For travelling I wore my new white wool coat with matching hat.

We had five wonderful days in London, spending hours in the parks, castles and museums. When we arrived home we found Ben's mum had filled our cupboards with food and given us four lovely Yorkshire blankets, something we really needed. Another box was waiting for us, containing a pretty grey-blue tea service from Betty. Sadly, I was never to see Betty again. She died very young from cancer.

• • •

Ben and I began our new life together. He went back on his five-day runs and I went back to work at the shop. Ann came over while Ben was away and told me Mum had apparently asked Aunty Ivy to find out the name of our wedding photographer. She wanted to get a photograph of me in my wedding dress — but not Ben.

The months passed quickly and we didn't hear from my parents. One day Ben and I were downtown. It was packed with people. We crossed a crosswalk without realizing that Dad had passed us going the other way. The light changed and suddenly I looked back and saw him. He waved and smiled and went on his way. Through Ann, I later heard he told Mum and Aunt Ivy that he had caught sight of me and that I looked prettier than ever.

When Ben and I had been married ten months, a terrible urge came over me — I wanted a baby. We had talked about this before we married, and we intended to wait at least two years, to save a deposit for a house of our own. The doctor also said I might need surgery before I could get pregnant. So I was determined to put it out of my mind.

When I went back to work, the general manager asked me to fill in for the manager of another shop while she was on holiday. I popped in to let her know who was taking her place, and I recognized her the minute I walked through the door. She used to pass us every day with her elder sister while we waited for the school bus. Their dad was a very well known rag-and-bone merchant. He had a big horse and went around collecting throwaways, such as clothing and iron beds. It was a good business. They had a big house down the tree-lined St. George's Road. When I told her my surname, she immediately asked if my husband was a marine engineer named Ben. I said yes, and she told me her sister had planned to marry him. Though I had been with him for nearly four years, I had never heard this before.

"Oh, they went out on and off for two or maybe three months," she said. "We all really liked him."

I couldn't wait to tell Ben. He laughed and explained he'd been quite young when he started going to sea. He and the sister had met at a dance and he had dated her on and off for a while, never planning to get married. It had been very different with me, he said. Six weeks after he met me, he knew for sure I was the one he wanted to marry.

Not long afterwards, I was told I might be transferred temporarily to a shop near where my old college boyfriend John lived. I said I could only do it if it fit in with Ben's schedule. All I could think about was what a coincidence it would be if I accidentally bumped into my ex. I had liked him very much, but the timing had never worked out for us. I found myself getting quite excited at the thought of seeing him again. But it turned out Ben would be home during those dates, and he couldn't understand why I would even think about going out of town.

I always felt slightly guilty when I thought of past episodes in my life, even the simple crush I'd had on Joyce's brother Gordon. Did other women think about their ex-boyfriends? I asked myself if the guilt I felt was because all my life I'd had it drilled into me that I should behave and obey. I couldn't talk to anyone about what I was thinking. They might think I was a bad person.

• • •

Joyce and Laurie got married three months after we did. I went to the wedding on my own, as Ben was away. After the ceremony Joyce's mum asked me to come back home with the family to celebrate. I had a drink or two and found I was getting giggly, so I went outside and sat in the conservatory. Along came Gordon, and we ended up having the longest conversation we'd had in all the years I'd been going to their house. He asked about my husband and all sorts of things. I told him we were settling down nicely and I was quite over the crush I'd had on him most of my life. He never knew. We laughed and laughed.

The drink had begun to give me a headache, so I decided I should go. He helped me on with my coat and offered to take me home. I was glad for his company. I wasn't used to having a drink, never mind two. We walked the two short streets to my place, and I thanked him. He gave me a big hug and kissed me goodnight. I went inside and fell on the couch. I was so glad I'd told him — business closed.

Settling Down

My stomach and peptic ulcer started acting up a bit more than usual, and I was sick every morning before I went to work. It suddenly dawned on me that my period hadn't come. Maybe I was pregnant! Ben got very excited, but we decided we wouldn't say anything till we were sure. Two and a half months later my doctor confirmed it. He suggested I go into a hospital or private home for my first birth, especially as my blood was Rh negative.

Joyce was pregnant too, and had moved back home to her mum and dad's. With five children, her mum had a lot of knowledge to pass on. All I knew was what we had done with Babs. I didn't want to burden Ben's mum, as she seemed quite frail. We told Ben's family, and they were as excited as we were. I wondered how Dad and Mum would have felt if they'd known.

One morning while alone in the house I had a severe vomiting attack. The contents of my stomach were black, so I knew I was having a hemorrhage. I went straight to the doctor. By the time I got there my neck was black and blue from the straining and I felt bruised all over. The doctor said that after a hemorrhage the ulcer often begins to clear up, but as it turned out I would need to wait two years more for that to happen. Joyce said she couldn't remember ever having gone on a bus with me without my feeling sick, having to get off early, and throwing up in the gutter.

In better news, Ben said we had finally saved enough money to put down a deposit on a house of our own. We had really enjoyed living in our flat, often chatting with the young tenant, Margaret, who lived in the bedsitter (bachelor apartment) next to our kitchen. There was also a small, delicate lady who lived in the other bedsitter down the hall, but she seemed to run away every time she saw anybody. We were ready to start looking for our own place, and we needed to find something before the baby was born.

Frank suggested we buy their mum's house. I could see it was a good idea financially, as we would save the realty cost, and we would be able to move in before the baby arrived. Frank said he would leave us the TV, something we didn't have and maybe wouldn't be able to afford for a while. However, I was somewhat disappointed that Ben agreed before we had even discussed it or had a chance to look at homes. There was nothing more to say. It seemed Ben had already decided it was best for all of us.

Frank moved his mum to a nice house close to his work. He had become a partner in a well-known removal company, so he would be home more often than before. I felt sorry for Frank. With his brothers away so often, he had always taken on the responsibility of looking after their mum.

When Joe left the Army we thought he would be around for a while, but a few weeks later he told Frank he was getting married. None of us knew he had even been seeing anyone.

"You'll never believe who he's marrying," Frank announced in dismay.

I thought for a minute and said, "Frances, your aunt."

"How on earth did you guess that?" he asked.

The last time we had all been together, right after Joe came home, I'd noticed a look, a kind of twinkle in their eyes as they looked at one another. Observing people was something I had done in my nursing, and it was a habit I never lost.

Frances was their aunt by marriage, the widow of Ben's mum's youngest brother, a well-known fisherman. One of her daughters had been in my class at school and had played on the rounders team with me. I recalled her telling us that her dad was very ill and was having stomach surgery. Unfortunately, he died during the operation.

Joe had always hung out at their house when he was on leave, helping with renovations.

The night before Joe and Frances's wedding, Ben went out to celebrate. After midnight, I heard a banging on the door. It was Frank and his friend, carrying Ben between them. While Ben had been enjoying his vodka and lime, his cousins had stopped adding the lime and given him straight vodka, a prank they had often pulled in the past. He was flat out, so Frank and his friend just sat him in the easy chair. He was a dead weight; we couldn't even remove his raincoat. Not long after they left, he got sick and rolled onto the floor. Being pregnant, I had no intention of even trying to lift him. I cleaned up the mess, put a pillow under his head and a blanket over him, and went to bed.

The next morning, the wedding day, he looked as white as a ghost and was as stiff as a board. I told him it served him right. He knew how his cousins always forced drinks on him. He wasn't feeling at all well when we reached the church. The priest shook hands with him and said, "You must be Joe's brother, you look so much alike." I laughed to myself, thinking, I hope Joe doesn't look much like Ben today.

It took quite a while for the hangover to wear off. Ben definitely was not up to dancing, so I had a dance with Frank. I realized this was the first time I had been to a dance in my life. Maybe, I thought, I should do this more often.

Motherhood

With a child on the way, I was glad to have a place of our own. We bought a nice bedroom suite and a cot for the baby, while downstairs we had a small melamine table with two chairs and a cozy maroon loveseat, where we could sit and watch our small black-and-white TV. The floors were all lino — easy to wash and keep clean — but the wallpaper in the sitting room was old-fashioned, and I decided to change it. I wanted a modern look, with green on the chimney wall and yellow on the other three.

When I stripped the walls, I found there were nine layers of paper! Gran and Mum had always said never to paper on top of wallpaper, mainly because the seams showed through. I had watched them as a little girl, but this was the first time I had attempted to do it on my own. We had no stepstool, but I had a tea chest, old but sturdy, that was big enough to stand on.

Ben walked in just as I reached the chimney wall. "What on earth are you doing up there on that chest!" he exclaimed. "You could break your neck and damage the baby."

Having watched Grandma, in her seventies, balance on a plank on the upstairs landing, I wasn't a bit scared to climb. It was just what we did — we didn't even think about it. Ben suggested I show him how to wallpaper and he would try to finish it for me. He did a good job, too.

One night I suggested we go see the new Frankenstein movie with Boris Karloff. I loved scary films. When we got to the cinema, Ben pulled me aside and told me his mum didn't think it was a good idea for me to see this kind of movie. It was too scary; I might damage the baby. "What if the baby is born with two heads or something?" he asked. He offered to take me to the theatre opposite and promised I could see this one later.

Exactly a week after the due date, I felt the first pain at midnight. By lunchtime the pains were still every ten minutes, so the home advised Ben to bring me in. The home was Poperinge, in Cottinham, the same place Joyce had had her daughter Karen. After I was examined they told Ben to go home. In those days they didn't want the fathers around, and it looked to be a long labour.

I had a room to myself but I was checked on regularly. As the hours went by, I wondered if anything was ever going to happen. The pain had continued to come every ten minutes, and I was exhausted. That night at eleven fifteen, I was finally taken to the delivery room, where my doctor was waiting. I was given a mask, which seemed to ease the pain. Ben would be worried, I thought, not knowing how long this would go on. At eleven thirty I was given a drop or two of ether. All I could hear was someone saying, "Eleven thirty-five, and this boy should be named."

"Long Tom" was the answer.

I felt so dozy. The nurse told me I was going back to my room. My baby, she said, was going to the nursery and I would see him in the morning. The doctor said, "I told you it was going to be a boy."

Still dozy, I said, "You mean that was my son?" I was so sleepy I couldn't take it all in.

I had a good night's sleep and woke up to a terrible noise of screaming babies. It was feeding time and I was right next door to the nursery, which at that time had twenty-seven babies. A few were going home that day, and I would be moved to a room for four people.

Born October 27, 1957, our son weighed seven pounds three ounces and was very long. His head was shaped like an egg and he had a few hairs, so white you could hardly see them. I couldn't help thinking, Thank goodness we didn't see the Frankenstein movie. Otherwise Ben would have blamed Boris Karloff for sure! The nurse explained that our son's head shape was from pressure during the birth and should be normal within two or three days.

I was told I had one stitch, or as we would say nowadays, one suture. It would be six days before I was able to leave my bed to go to the toilet, which meant using a bedpan in front of three strangers. There was one thing I finally believed after seeing the lady opposite me struggling away on a bedpan – I definitely was not deformed, as my mum had said. For the first time in my life I was convinced I was normal.

Our baby, cute in his green jacket, was now named Long Tom. After three days his head returned to normal and he was a bonny little boy. One day the nurse brought him to me tightly wrapped in a blanket. He felt much heavier. When I tried to start the feeding, I couldn't get him to nurse. Something wasn't right. Suddenly the girl on the opposite bed shouted, "You have my baby!" In came a nurse saying, "Here's your little Long Tom." From then on I always double-checked the wrist ID.

I wasn't allowed to walk around until the ninth day, and when I did my knees were so weak I could hardly walk. We were in the home for fourteen days. They taught us how to bathe, change and feed our babies. Husbands, though not others, were encouraged to visit every day. Ben came to see me, and as he left the building the first person he bumped into was my mum. He had placed a birth announcement at the newspaper office, so that was how she'd known.

Right away Mum began screaming at him, saying he had taken her daughter miles away from them. Ridiculous, considering we were living in the same house Ben had lived in when we were going out together, about ten miles away from my parents. I'd known that if we had a boy they might be very upset, knowing how much Dad had always wished for a son.

Later, Ann turned up at the home with a gift from them; they had asked her, through Aunt Ivy, to bring it to us. It was a very nice knitted shawl and a white baby jacket and booties. I asked Ann to pass on our thanks through Aunt Ivy. I said if they wanted to change things, they only had to tell us.

At last we were allowed to go home. My legs were so weak I had to hang onto the pram. We chose Andrew for a name — short, simple and nice. Mum and baby settled into a routine, though feeding him was a struggle. I had bleeding nipples and an abscess, and I was in agony. I had to pump my milk and feed Andrew with a bottle. I had so much milk, my blouses were always soaking wet.

After being away from his ship for almost a full month, Ben went back to his five-day trips. I seemed to be on twenty-four-hour shifts with Andrew, and I grew tired and weepy. On his next day home Ben said he would take care of Andrew and I could go downtown and buy something new to wear. It was the first time I'd left the baby since he was born, and I missed him so much. Ben made me a nice cup of tea when I got home. I couldn't stop crying. Andrew had been quite happy with his dad and I'd needed that break.

A couple of weeks later I twisted my foot when I jumped out of a chair too quickly. I was in a lot of pain and my foot really swelled up. The phone was about three bus stops away, but I didn't want to ask anybody for help. The pain got much worse, so I finally went to my next-door neighbour, Mrs. P. She offered to take Andrew while I went to the hospital. I hobbled to the bus, and luckily it dropped me off near the infirmary. It turned out I had broken a bone in my foot. I had to wear a cast for eight weeks, but the cast had a heel so I was able to get around, and Ben was home every few days. I realized, thanks to Mrs. P, that no matter how independent I wanted to be, there would always be times when I needed someone's help.

Ben was determined to find another job, one that would enable him to be with us all the time, and he found work by the dock. It was quite a way to go on his bike and the salary was much less than he had earned at sea, but he was home with us. He would leave in the morning at six thirty and wouldn't get home till seven or seven thirty at night.

Washing and drying the laundry took most of a day without a washer or even a wringer. The cotton nappies we used in those days had to be soaked, washed and boiled in a steel bucket on the gas stove. Wringing them out with your hands was hard work. If it was sunny, we could dry them on the washing line in the garden. Otherwise it was on a clothes horse around the fireplace.

We didn't go to the pictures anymore, and we wouldn't even think of asking anyone to babysit for us. In the 1950s, if you had children you stayed at home. It did seem like all work and no play — rather, that was what we called responsibility. We visited the parks often to feed the ducks, and we spent lots of time in our sizeable garden. Ann visited me nearly every week, and on weekends we went to church with Ben's mum and Frank.

I always appreciated the way our doctors and nurses used to look after us back then. If you were really sick, they came to your home. If you were pregnant, maternity nurses checked on you through each month. If the baby was born at home, they came twice a day for two full weeks after the birth. They bathed the baby, checked the mum thoroughly, and then went through all the routines she needed to know to handle her baby. We had clinics to provide concentrated orange juice and iron pills. During the war, juices had not been available to everyone, only to expectant mothers.

Though I knew I was being well looked after, there were times when I felt a little lost. I realized it was because I didn't have my own family around me. They were not there to answer simple questions or share the excitement at Andrew's milestones. I always thanked God for Joyce, though. I knew I couldn't go wrong following her advice. I was astonished to hear she was potty training Karen already, and by nine months she was out of nappies. I did what she did with Andrew, not expecting it to work with a boy. But it worked. Nine months old, and he was wearing underwear under his tiny trousers instead of the bulky nappies. It came from spending every minute of your time with your child, learning their routines as they grew.

The nickname Long Tom fit Andrew well. At first I bathed him in a regular-sized baby bath in front of the fire; we just had coal fires, no central heating. This didn't last very long, because his legs were soon too long to sit in it, and I had to use the kitchen sink. By the time he was four months old I was buying him little boys' pants meant to fit a one-year-old.

He was sitting up straight at four months. I would lay him down flat and the next minute he would pull himself straight up again. I couldn't keep him down. A neighbour who had a boy the same age said he shouldn't be doing that till he was six months, but the doctor said some babies were just ahead of others and not to worry.

Andrew crawled early and would pull himself up on the edge of the couch, walk to the end, and then plunk down on his bottom. At nine months he was walking on his own. I didn't dare take my eyes off him. No matter what toys he had, he was quite happy playing with a saucepan full of pegs. Frank and his mum loved him. Frank bought him a big pedal car for Christmas, and he spent most of his days driving up and down the garden. He was a happy little boy.

• • •

Frank, having been an instructor at Sandhurst Military College, offered to give Ben driving lessons in his car, a small blue Fiat with a canvas top. Wherever I have lived, I have never found a place whose driving tests are as hard as England's. For the final test, after the driving was done, they took you to a quiet place and grilled you with verbal questions. No ticking off boxes as they do today. Ben passed his driving test, and a few weeks later Frank brought the car round to our house and gave it to him as a present. Frank had seen a racing car he wanted to buy.

Ben did a lot around the house at weekends. He flushed all the doors, which made them much more modern. He added more kitchen cupboards and, because I loved colour, painted them pale blue with tiny red knobs. I helped by wallpapering the two bedrooms. His mum bought us a large maroon rug for Christmas, and since we didn't have a vacuum, once a month I hung it on the washing line and beat it with a special tool. It made me think of home, and how that had been one of my chores to earn pocket money.

Things were going along nicely, and we talked about having another baby. Then one night Ben came home looking very sad. His company had told everyone they would be laid off within three weeks. The country was going into a depression, and things were not looking good. We had to face the fact that his qualifications would take him back to sea. It seemed that, due to the depression, all the coastal ships were already full. The only ones hiring were the supertankers. Of those, Esso was the only company that guaranteed leave after six months. When your time was up, they would fly you home from wherever you happened to be.

It was too much for me to take in. The last time he had been away for six months, when we were going out, I'd had a career to keep me busy. This time it would be different. I would be on my own with our son, and I would have total responsibility for our home. I was scared.

Alone Again

Saying goodbye was heartbreaking. At not quite two years old, Andrew was too young to understand why his daddy wasn't there anymore. I was in a daze. I couldn't get it into my head that Ben was going to be away for half a year.

It wouldn't help either of us for me to sit and mope about. I had to keep busy. We spent a lot of time in the garden, Andrew driving his car up and down while I planted flowers and vegetables. Almost every night I wrote to Ben and then knitted until late in the evening. There was no nylon wool in those days, and if a baby spilled milk on his jacket, it became matted. The jackets had to be replaced regularly, and they were too expensive to keep buying.

One day I went outside to get some coal to light our fire, and as I lifted the lid I saw three large rats running around inside. I dropped the lid and screamed so loud Mrs. P came running out, followed by her husband. He brought newspaper and matches and lit a fire in the hole at the end of the bin. Out came the rats, one by one, at the other end. Our other neighbour kept rabbits, so the rats were probably after their food. I hadn't seen rats, especially that size, since the war years.

I would have to get used to taking care of things myself. Ben's mum and Frank lived across the city, and we didn't have a phone. I couldn't expect them to be at my beck and call. My biggest fear was electricity. Ben had told me that if a fuse in the stove or a light blew, there were different sized amps of wire which had to be twisted into holes. I wasn't sure I'd remember what size was for what. When it did happen, I don't know how many times I closed my eyes. Once the wire was in I had to fit the plug into the proper place. Closing my eyes didn't help at all. I held my breath as well, until I was sure I wouldn't be electrocuted.

I spent the weekends as usual with Ben's mum and Frank. Sometimes we went to the seaside or to see the gliders in Frank's car. We loved the beach and ice cream. I offered to do the laundry for Ben's mum. If I kept extra busy, I didn't feel so lonely.

I decided to take Andrew downtown to show him the docks where the small ships came in. We crossed the road to get on the bus, and in front of us was an older man wearing a flat cap. "Mummy, do I have a daddy like that?" asked Andrew.

The tears rolled down my cheeks. "Yes, darling," I said. "You have a very nice daddy. In a few weeks he'll be coming home to see us again."

Ben came home in time for Christmas, and Andrew had no problem recognizing his dad again. It was a nice long leave and we made every minute count. Before Ben was to go back, I began to suspect I might be expecting again, as I had been vomiting in the mornings. Ben was very pleased.

Just before Ben left, he said to Andrew, "While I'm away you're the little man of our house. Please take good care of Mummy." After that I noticed that every time Andrew went out to play with Mrs. P's little boy, he would be back five minutes later. "That was quick," I would say. "I thought you went out to play for a while?"

Then he would say, "I just came in to see if you were all right."

If my dates were correct, Ben would be home for the birth. Mrs. P said she would help out, and I was very pleased to have someone to rely on. Funnily enough, once again I found out Joyce was also expecting around the same time.

Ben really liked his job on the supertankers. He was a First Class Engineer and he had his own room and office. They had movies and a swimming pool on board, plus they received a very good wage. I had already begun to see in him the urge to move around. When he and his brothers were young, their mum had moved them several times, not always to a better place. As the boys grew, they joked that she should buy a caravan so she could move somewhere new every month. I realized Ben was born with a similar restlessness.

For what would probably be our last outing before the baby came, I decided to take Andrew to the docks. He saw some small fishing boats coming in and started laughing and jumping. In his excitement he bumped into a woman who was crossing the bridge. "Lady, lady," he said. "Nice boats." She put her hands on his shoulders and looked at me. It was Mum.

"So this is my grandson," she said. "What a lovely little boy."

I didn't know what to say. She asked me how I was doing. I told her I was expecting the baby in the next week or two. Then she implied Barbara might like to come and see me. I said she was welcome, that we would love to see her too. We said bye and went on our ways.

It had been five years since I had seen my parents. Babs had been almost six when I left. I had only seen her once since then, when she came into the shop where I worked in town. She had been wearing a green organdy dress and a matching bow. I had always thought she was so pretty, with her red hair and her face covered in freckles. Now she would be almost eleven.

Not long after that, the baby came. It was exactly midnight when I felt the first pain, and they got worse quickly. Ben went to call my midwife from the nearest phone box. It was only three or four bus stops away, but at that hour he had to walk — or rather, run. The midwife had a thirty-minute journey. When she arrived, the pains were every ten minutes, but because my first labour had lasted twenty-four hours, she didn't expect this baby to take less than twelve hours. She said she'd be back the next morning at nine o'clock.

The pains didn't stop, and at six thirty my waters broke. Ben banged on the bedroom wall and Mrs. P came over immediately. Ben ran out the door in his slippers, back to the phone. I went back to bed, and ten minutes later the baby was there. Just before it came out, I said to Mrs. P, "It's a girl, isn't it?"

"How do you know that?" she said. "I can only see the top of the head."

"I just know," I said. I was right. It was a girl with dark blonde hair.

The front door opened with a bang and Ben galloped up the stairs. "I thought I heard a baby cry when I opened the front door."

"You did," I said. "We have a daughter this time." His eyes lit up when he saw her.

Andrew had slept through all the noise, for which I was grateful, and was very happy to see his sister. The doctor came and said my regular nurse would be with me for the next two weeks. Our little girl had blue eyes with long dark eyelashes. We named her Ann.

· · ·

Alone again, I settled into a new routine, this time with two children. Andrew was happy with his little sister, and I could see he was going to be the daddy of the house again. I kept myself busy by renovating our bathroom. When I showed Mum and Frank, Frank said, "Who did you get to do this for you?"

I told him I had done it myself.

"Who do you think you're kidding? A man must have done the bath to start with."

Typical man, I thought. Can't believe a woman is capable of doing anything. Andrew said straight away, "My mummy did those pictures in our bathroom. I carried the wood from the shop, on Ann's pram." Finally Frank admitted I had done a very good job.

I went to visit my family, and things went well. Yet I was always on my guard for any domination from my mum. I expected them to be respectful to Ben also when he came home; I didn't intend to have any more nonsense in our lives. It was nice to see them again, and Babs got on well with Andrew. When Ben came home, they genuinely seemed happy to see him. He and Dad got back to chatting about the sea. I was glad, but also sad for all the time we'd lost.

At sixty-eight Ben's mum moved to a rest home by the seaside. Frank took us to see her every two weeks in his shiny new car, which Andrew loved, and we would drive her along the seafront. She would sleep until we got to the café for her favourite bacon sandwich, then sleep all the way back. When we got back to the home, she always said she'd had a wonderful day.

Frank began to think of selling their house. His business partners, Peter and Dianne, lived in a huge house on the office grounds. They told Frank he was welcome to share, since it was so big. Peter and his grandfather had known Frank since he was a little boy and thought the world of him. Frank ran the business, Peter drove the big vans, and Dianne ran the office. It worked out fine for all of them.

• • •

Every summer the Travellers parked their caravans in the large fields and parks at the back of our garden, where army barracks had been during the war. They usually stayed two or three weeks. Sometimes they knocked on our doors and asked to fill their pots with water at our sinks. One day I walked into my kitchen to find a man already at the sink filling his bucket. I hadn't heard a knock on the door. Up to that day I had never locked my door unless I was going out somewhere.

The Gypsies were quite pushy when selling their pegs and lucky lavender. They did well with the pegs, because everyone hung out their washing. Whether the lavender was lucky was a matter of opinion, but you would be told if you didn't buy any that you would have bad luck. Most people bought it. I think they were scared not to.

When Ann was three weeks old, we all took a walk in the park. Andrew wanted to go on the swings, but they were all taken by the Gypsy children, happily swinging up in the air. They were girls around thirteen, in dresses that kept blowing over their heads. Ben's face went red. None of them were wearing any underwear. We hurried off with Andrew and the pram. I felt sad for them because they looked so dirty. Their caravans had no showering facilities. Their clothes were mostly hand-me-downs. Yet they seemed very happy.

Moving House

After four and a half years in our home, Ben suggested, completely unexpectedly, that we look for a bigger house. He thought it would be nice for Ann to have her own room. We decided to look around Elloughton, a village near Brough, where Mum had worked during the war.

We found a beautiful bungalow, modern and comfortable, with a farm behind it. There were three bedrooms, a long sitting room with an L-shaped dining area, and a kitchen with fitted cabinets in a pale grey-blue. Though modern, it had no central heating, only a gas fire. There was a big garden in the front, back and down the side that would keep both me and the children very busy.

Ben dug the garden over and put up a swing out back for the children to play on. Then it was time for another six-month stint at sea. The kids and I were in the garden every day. We made a curved rockery right around the patio. Andrew and Ann loved piling up the stones, and our new cat, Tinker, used to hide behind the rockery to catch birds. The children wanted to grow carrots as well as flowers, so we made a big vegetable patch at the back of the garden.

Andrew began school at age four and a half on a lovely late summer day. We told Ann he would go in the morning and come home for lunch, and then we would pick him up in the afternoon. No matter how many times we explained this, she always cried, missing her brother so. Perhaps she thought he would disappear as her daddy had. She began to sob so much that I had to keep stopping the pram to cuddle her.

As we headed home, I noticed her breathing wasn't good and she seemed to be turning blue. I ran in to call the doctor — thankfully by that time we had a phone — and he arrived in a matter of minutes. By then she had collapsed and needed an adrenalin injection. From that day on, she had very bad asthma attacks and had to have an injection almost every month.

I thought of my mum. With Dad away for years, she'd had to be responsible for everything; now I was the same. Maybe that was why she was so dominant. I began to feel very sorry for her, but least she'd had her family all around her.

In the meantime, it was no use feeling sorry for myself. During the week Frank either popped in for a cup of tea or rang up to see how we were. Rita next door told me to call her when Ann was sick, especially at nighttime. At times I did, and she would come in and cuddle Ann while we waited for the doctor. I decorated a different room every six months to make it look nice for Ben. I also bought a knitting machine from a friend at a good price and started knitting sweaters non-stop for the children.

One day a man came to read the gas meter; he was a former bus conductor I had known years ago. While he was doing the reading, I saw a bit of dust around the telephone and panicked. Hoping he hadn't seen it, I ran to get the furniture polish. I was so afraid he might think I was a dirty person. Then I sat down and had a cup of tea, and I cried my eyes out. What was happening to me? Was I going nutty?

On my next visit to the doctor, I told him how I was feeling. He told me I was doing a wonderful job of coping, and that cleaning was obviously my way of keeping busy. He suggested getting in touch with Shirley, who was also having difficulties dealing with her husband's absences. That I did, and we found we very much enjoyed each other's company. I also talked to Joyce. They had three girls now, and I knew how busy she was. Her husband Laurie was soon transferred to Doncaster, but we saw each other regularly until they moved.

• • •

Ben had bought a black shiny Renault Dauphine, a three-gear car, but it sat in the garage while he was away. He had showed me how to check the oil and tires, and said he would teach me to drive. The next time he was home, Ben, Frank, and I went for a spin with me in the driver's seat. An oncoming car approached us down a narrow country road, and Ben yelled at me, "Stop, you silly bugger!"

When the car had passed, I opened the door, got out, and slammed it shut as hard as I could. "Drive the bloody thing yourself!" I said.

That was my first and last driving lesson with Ben. We had never sworn at each other before. Frank took over my lessons. He was strict, as Ben had warned, and there were times when I wanted to pour a pot of tea on his head afterwards. Yet his teaching made me a careful driver.

Ben decided to go back to college to get his First Class Certificate for motor ships. He was home for a while, and though he had a lot of studying to do, it was lovely to be together. I couldn't see him working anywhere but at sea. He had the best of both worlds, travelling all over the world and then coming home to a family. Also, they paid a decent wage now. Before he left again, he came up with something that blew my mind – immigrating to Australia.

He had spent about three weeks in Sydney, years before, and said Perth was also very nice. We could immigrate for ten pounds each as long as we stayed three years. I had my doubts. It was so far away and we would be leaving everyone behind. Then again, I would go to the ends of the earth with him, provided we were happy. Every letter we wrote for the next six months was about Australia, and we agreed it was the place to go. But when he came back, he decided he didn't want to go, and his decision was final.

Ben's ship was going into dry dock in Amsterdam, so we decided I would take Andrew and Ann there and we'd have a family holiday. Amsterdam was wonderful, and we all enjoyed ourselves. I had only been back a few days when I began to feel depressed and frightened, with a feeling of death all around me. I wondered if I was going to die. I began to worry about the children. What would become of them if anything happened to me? A few evenings later when the children were in bed, there was a knock on the door. It was my mum. She told me Uncle Ted had died. Now I knew why I had been feeling that way. We had always been close.

When we arrived at Grandma's for the service, both Gran and Aunt Ivy gave us all big hugs. I took the children across the road to Ann's mum, who had offered to take care of them; Ann and her sisters were there and so was Babs. Uncle Ted was in his coffin in Gran's front room. As I walked in, there was Iris bending over his coffin, kissing him goodbye. I took his hand. It was so cold, but he looked very peaceful. We had lived all those years with this quiet, loving uncle. It was the first time I had ever been to a cremation. The coffin, surrounded by flowers, disappeared slowly through the curtains.

Soon after Ben's next departure, I began to feel sickly. My stomach was acting up, perhaps from the stress of Uncle Ted's death and Ben's regular absences. I was vomiting every morning, and I realized I might be pregnant again. We had wanted a third child but had decided to wait a bit because of Ann's asthma.

I was going to have this baby at home again, and if things worked out Ben might be home at the same time. When I went into labour, as usual around midnight, I received a telegram from Ben saying his ship might be delayed a day or two. My labour stopped. The doctor said, "This baby's going to wait for his dad." The nurse said, "If he's home, he'd better not get in my way or I'll kick him under the bed."

On the morning of the third day Ben rang at five o'clock, saying he would be home in three hours and would like to take Andrew to school. However, he had to return to the ship by eleven thirty to fully sign off. I was in labour again when I put the phone down. Ben and I had a couple of hours together before he went back to the ship. As he left, he tapped my tummy and said, "Don't come, baby, until I get back."

The doctor came, followed by the nurse. "This is the day, now that Daddy's home," said the doctor. "I'll come back after lunch. If something happens, call me immediately." I was still having pains, but nothing seemed to be happening, so I told the nurse Ben would be home any minute and she should go for lunch.

Ben arrived while I was making lunch. We sat down to eat and the pains began coming fast. I sent Ann to the lounge with a book to read to her teddy bear (not that she could read, but she usually showed him the pictures), while I went and lay down in bed. Ten minutes later, Ben saw the baby. He had to guide it out right away. It seemed so small – I couldn't even see its legs.

Quickly Ben covered us up with a blanket and grabbed the phone. The doctor's wife answered, quite flustered. She said the doctor was on his way, but she would send his partner immediately in case of a delay. Their office was very near, so the partner arrived in five minutes, wanting to know why we were on our own. My doctor and nurse walked in right behind him, before we had chance to answer. We didn't even know yet if it was a boy or girl.

It was a tiny little girl, six pounds three ounces. She had red hair the same shade as Barbara's. She was born on March 17, 1964, Saint Patrick's Day. Ben was thrilled to bits, never having expected that he would deliver her. Once everything was done, Andrew and Ann got to hold the baby. Frank came later in the evening and arranged to bring his mum at the weekend. Mum and Dad brought Barbara the next lunchtime. It was great to be together at a time like this, a new beginning for all of us.

We called her Margaret. Mum and Dad didn't come to the christening, as it was a Catholic church. Frank was her godfather, as he was to all three of them. I wouldn't have had it any other way. He was always like a second father to them all.

Margaret grew into a very bonny baby. Like Andrew and Ann, she adjusted to her dad's coming and going. She reminded me so much of Barbara when she was a baby. Ann still had her asthma attacks, yet I felt fine, coping with the three of them. They seemed to keep each other busy, especially outside on the swing. It was much easier for me somehow.

I took the children to see Gran and Aunty Ivy. The first thing Gran said to me was that I should have had someone looking after me when I gave birth – it wasn't a job for a man. I told her it was just something that had happened when no one else was there. The same had happened with Ann. As for looking after me, Ben had been looking after me ever since we got married. No one else had. His family too had always been there for me. Surprisingly, I was able to tell Gran just what I thought. I had an excellent doctor who checked me every day and a terrific nurse who was there every day for two weeks. Ben coped well with the children and the meals. What more could I have wished for?

• • •

Ben left again and life had to go on as usual. The next time he came home, he had another shock for us all. He'd had an offer to become a boiler inspector, a chance for a job on land for good. He had been in touch with the company and they had asked him to go to London for an interview. Evidently he thought the salary was good, and every year he would be provided with a new car.

He had never mentioned anything of this in his letters. As with the Australia plan, everything was sorted before I even knew where we were going. My mind was going haywire. We would be leaving our families and a home we loved. Andrew would have to leave his school.

Ben believed it was a good job, and we would be together for good, so off he went to London to find out all about it. The look on Frank's face when we told him was one of bewilderment. I told him about Australia, which we hadn't mentioned to anyone before. Frank said, "Maybe he'll change his mind again." But I wasn't so sure this time.

Ben was offered the job and given a choice of three cities: London, Stoke on Trent or Norwich. London was nice, but too expensive. We definitely couldn't afford to live there. Stoke on Trent was smoky, which was not good for Ann's asthma. Ben thought I would love Norwich. He had it all worked out. We could put the house up for sale, and he would go ahead of us.

Frank dreaded having to tell his mum, and I was hesitant to speak to my family. Ben said they could all come and visit. At least it wouldn't be as far as Australia, I thought. In my heart, all I knew was it would never be the same. But Ben had made up his mind, and I knew he wouldn't change it this time. It was only the thought of how much I had loved Norwich years ago that kept me going.

We had been in our first house four and a half years and the same amount of time in the second. I hoped the next one would be forever. I prayed that Ben would be happy in his new job. We would miss our families so much.

• • •

Ben found us a bungalow on a new estate, similar to what we had before but slightly smaller. Every day for weeks I rearranged the furniture while Ben was at work. He said, "One day I might come home and find my shirts in one place." I papered the walls and painted the kitchen doors three different colours. We had central heating, which was cozy, and there were trees everywhere behind the house.

Andrew and Ann went to a Catholic school. Margaret and I walked them to the corner of the village and saw them onto the little school bus every morning. The village was quaint, with a few shops and a post office. For the first three months I worried I had said something to upset the post lady, as she wasn't at all friendly. It struck me years later, when I came across the same thing, that she hadn't been able to understand me. In England you can travel ten miles and find a new accent. All the different shires sound different, and Yorkshire is totally different from the rest of England. After about three months, the post lady became very friendly.

• • •

We made friends with our neighbours, who also had children, and after we had been there a while they suggested we take turns babysitting, maybe once a month. This was something new for us. Only twice had we ever left Andrew, for Joe's wedding and for a special St. Patrick's Day dance. Now we could occasionally go to a movie or pop over to the local pub for a drink. We also decided to get a puppy for the children, a black Labrador we called Sooty. As he grew, he loved us all, especially the children. He didn't seem to like men and barked all the time if they came near us.

Mum, Dad and Barbara came to visit. We went to Yarmouth, a beautiful town known for its beaches. Ben had work to do, but he dropped us off for the day. As we were about to leave, Barbara said she had to run into the bathroom because she had forgotten her deodorant. I went after her to tell her to hurry, only to find her holding up her dress and spraying herself. Heading for the car, she began to walk funny. A few minutes later, she realized she had sprayed herself with hairspray and not deodorant, and her legs were all sticky. We all burst out laughing.

Barbara had just reached eighteen and could legally drink. She told me she went drinking with her friends a lot. I asked her how Mum and Dad reacted to that, especially when she said she stayed out late. Her reply was that they couldn't do a thing about it. She was of legal age, and she had told them they weren't going to do to her what they had done to her sister. I was pleased to hear she knew about the rules I'd lived under.

Norfolk was famous for its cider, so we all went to a pub, Babs telling us she could drink anyone under the table. The cider was extra strong and very thick, almost like treacle, and came in a very small glass. Mum, like me, rarely drank, so we took one drink each. By the time I was a quarter through mine, I couldn't drink any more — it was far too strong for me. Mum was acting a bit strange and began to giggle. Babs finished hers and said she would be happy to finish off mine. We had to carry them both out to the car.

After they went home, I began to see a change in Ben. He was getting quite angry about our government and the economy. I said I thought we were doing fine. Every year we were given a new Mini car and we managed to save a little. What had we to complain about? We ended up having the first big argument we'd ever had. He didn't like my attitude, and I ended up telling him a few things I was upset about, things I had obviously stored up. We had been married ten years and were still madly in love. In my eyes, we hadn't wanted to waste our time together arguing. He said, "I wish you'd told me all this before. I would have tried to do better."

I felt terrible. How could I be mad with anyone so nice? I began to worry a bit when he was still grumpy about the government. Could it be that he was beginning to miss the family? Oh my goodness, was it the sea again? Oh please, God, I thought, don't let it be that. I had thought we were all happy and settled here.

Goodbye England

Something was definitely bothering Ben. When our washer needed replacing, he was angry that we would have to dip into our savings. I told him there wasn't enough money left over from weekly groceries and bills to buy items like that. We were lucky even to have savings. We didn't have credit cards in those days — it was pay cash or go without. Most people went without.

Our country was going down and no one was expecting any pay rises. Ben was sure it was our government. I waited for him to tell me what he wanted and didn't push. It didn't take long. I listened carefully, my heart going bumpety-bump. Yes, it was all about the country and the economy, but to my surprise it wasn't anything about going to sea, thank the Lord. He suggested we move to a better country. This time it was Canada.

He felt the children would have much better opportunities to go to university there. In our country it seemed you were able to get into university only if your family had a lot of money, like doctors or lawyers. I looked at Ben and thought about his education. He had done a seven-year apprenticeship, gone to college, and earned all his engineering certificates. No one could have done better. Myself, I couldn't have had a better college and nursing training.

I asked him what part of Canada he would choose to live in. I had heard it was very cold in some places, and there were places where you would have to learn French. Well, of course he had studied it well, as usual, and British Columbia was his choice. He even had an old BC Ferries job advert for marine engineers and had already written for information. Well, I thought, thank you for telling me. He was very excited about the area and about the fact that the job was at sea again but he would be home every day.

BC Ferries sent a letter saying the advert was quite old and all their jobs had been filled for the next six months. But they would offer him a job if he was able to support his family for that time, as his qualifications were just what they required.

He asked me to go with him to the Canadian immigration office in London. There our interviewer told him BC was in a depression, but he was impressed with Ben's qualifications and said Alberta was definitely looking for engineers. If Ben worked in Alberta, we could work our way to BC later if he was still interested in the ferries.

I knew straight away that Ben's mind was made up. I had seen all this excitement before. This time I was scared. It would be so far away from our families. Everyone — friends, family — was taken aback by our news. Joyce and Laurie said we needed our heads examined.

We signed up with Immigration to have our medicals. The only thing we were worried about was Ann and her asthma. She had outgrown it somehow in Norwich, perhaps because it was much drier there than northern England. The only time she had trouble was when we went back to visit family.

In addition to selling the house, we had to get rid of all our furniture. The removal company instructed us to have everything we were sending to Canada ready three months in advance. We were given a 5⊠ × 4⊠ box, in which I placed bedding and the Yorkshire blankets, my knitting machine, and toys for the children.

The saddest part of it all was that we couldn't take Sooty with us. Ben looked into trying to find another family for him. The animal shelter said they would do their best. When Ben took Sooty there and handed him over, Sooty gave him a look he never would forget. After that I didn't think we'd ever be able to face having another dog.

The buyer's money was late coming, so we changed the date from October. Next, the British pound was devalued, so we lost quite a sum of money. It struck me that if we had gone to Australia instead, our whole home and our electrical would have cost us only ten pounds each, as long as we stayed for three years. The airfare to Canada was £700 each, just one way. It was quite expensive to fly in those days, and we didn't want to go by boat in the winter.

Before leaving, we went to Norwich city centre to finish some business. The old houses looked so lovely next to the cathedral. I stood there remembering when I was sixteen and had come to visit my aunt and uncle. Suddenly Ben said, "Patsy, you know, we could buy any one of these old houses around the market." He rarely called me Patsy, but when he did it made me feel all cuddly. What was he saying? Was he going to change his mind now, after he had given up his job?

I told him I'd had a similar thought. I had noticed the hospital was just around the corner of the square, and I thought I could go back and finish my nursing when the children were grown.

I was shocked by his reaction — the look on his face and his reply. "I will never have you working again, no way. So we're going to Canada for sure." There was my answer.

After saying goodbye to all our friends and neighbours in Norwich, we took the children out of school and went to stay at Mum's place for our last week. She actually had Gran over, with Aunt Ivy and her boyfriend Arthur. Gran looked a bit lost and said she would really miss us. It was so strange after all these years to see her in Mum's house, and her and Mum actually speaking to each other. Babs was there, all grown up, with her boyfriend David, who seemed very nice. I was really going to miss Barbara. I couldn't help but think of the many things sisters do together. Ben's mum was there also, looking very sad. Frank dropped her off but didn't stay. I think he was too sad. We had already said goodbye to Joe and Frances.

Our last visit was to see Frank, Peter and Dianne, and their boys. This was Frank's new family. Every time I looked at Frank I felt choked. I couldn't believe we were leaving him behind. In fact, I still couldn't believe we were really going. But I was relieved to know he was living with a family who cared about him.

We said our final goodbyes and then it was time to go. The next day we would finally be starting our journey. I asked our family not to come to the railway station. It would have been too upsetting. As the train left Paragon Station, I wondered if we would ever see them again.

I kept wondering if we were doing the right thing. Should we have let Ben go ahead first? Well, we were all here now, taking the first steps together. I asked God to guide us and keep us all safe in this new country.

Canada
1967 – 1985

The End of the Earth

With all our worldly goods in a large suitcase each, we boarded the first plane any of us had ever been on. I held my breath as our Air Canada jet soared into the sky, leaving the beautiful greenery of England behind. I wondered how many years it would be before we came home again.

Our destination was Calgary, Alberta, but we landed first in Edmonton for Immigration. As we made our descent, I stared out the window searching for green fields. There was nothing green. Where the fields should have been, there were dark brown boxes. As we touched the runway, it was starting to sleet with snow. It was a long walk to the terminal, and the wind was blowing so hard we had to hold onto our hats. After going through Immigration, we ran back to the plane. It was thirty-nine degrees below zero. Oh dear God, what had we come to?

We landed in Calgary an hour later and took a taxi to a motel. It would be our home till Ben found a job. On December 5, 1967, we had our first meal in a Canadian restaurant, speaking to a real Canadian waitress — or so we thought. I assumed from her accent that she was Canadian, but she told us she had moved here from Aberdeen, Scotland, nine years before. She said she'd worked hard to lose her accent because nobody here could understand her. After we told her we had just arrived, she told us the depression in BC had spread to Alberta. If Ben didn't have a job within ten days, she said, we would be better off going back to England.

We settled into our motel hoping for the best. Our first trip out was to buy us all boots. It was snowing, but although it was cold the sun was shining. Our rooms were a good size, with cooking facilities, and I asked the children to draw some special pictures for Christmas and make some decorations. I started to bake cakes as usual, but everything I touched went flat. I wanted to cry.

Ben was asked to fly to Prince George, BC, to sort out his working qualifications, which would take two or three days. I was scared of being on my own, but I kept busy and bought some cookery books. I soon realized the flour here was different and needed baking powder. The next cake I baked actually turned out well.

I tried to get some drawing pins for the children's decorations, but it seemed nobody had any. I went to an office supplier, sure they must have some, but the clerk said they didn't carry them. I explained that in England everyone used them to pin up pictures, and began pressing my thumbs up. Seeing this she said, "Oh my goodness! You must mean thumb tacks."

Ben came back with good news — he would be starting a job after Christmas. Unfortunately he would have to work as a Second Class Engineer, since all immigrants had to retake the First Class test in Canada. Soon after, the company told Ben that instead of working in Calgary, he would be sent to Cold Lake. They would provide a home and a car and also arrange for a driver to take us there.

Cold Lake was a few hundred miles away, but Canadians were used to driving long distances. It snowed most of the way, and the wind howled. When we arrived at Cold Lake, all we could see was a big lake iced over, hence the name. It was so frozen you could drive your car over it for six months of the year. There was a main street of modular homes. We were given one opposite the RCMP building, with three bedrooms, one and a half bathrooms and a large basement. Next door was a young couple, and on their other side was a church minister. There was a large US Air Force base with its own shops and supplies that no one was allowed to enter.

We both had to get new driver's licenses. We weren't used to driving on snow and ice, though we soon learned. Our neighbour was extremely helpful and took us to the only place we could go for supplies, a small town eight miles away. It had a couple of furniture shops, a tiny Indigenous store with beautiful art and carvings, and a launderette. Most of the furniture in the first store was very old-fashioned, but the second store had two couches we liked, with side tables, lamps and cushions. I hadn't realized none of the houses had ceiling lights, so we needed end tables for lamps. For the bedrooms we bought a bed each, a set of drawers, and blankets with satin edges, hoping all our bedspreads were well on their way to Canada. We didn't buy a washer or a dryer, as I intended to use the launderette in town.

We bought an old Chevy for $200 from an American airman who was returning home. With Ben on shift work, I would be able to drive to the launderette and do all the shopping with Margaret while Andrew and Ann were in school. It was an eight-mile drive to the nearby town, and most of the time it was thirty-nine below.

On my first jaunt, I parked the car and carried the laundry bags to the launderette, only to find three drunken men lying across the steps. I was scared to climb over them with Margaret, so I turned around and went home. I did the washing by hand. The second and third time I went, it was exactly the same. I was not going to risk disturbing any drunks on the steps with Margaret around. From then on I did it all by hand, and Ben helped me wring out all the big bedding. We didn't have any carpets and a lot of snow came in with our boots, but it was easy to mop up. That seemed to be our life. We didn't go outside much — it was too cold. Luckily, the school was close.

We tried ice fishing. Drilling through the ice was very different, but each time we did catch fish. One night our neighbour, who fished regularly, brought us three enormous pike. Ben was at work till eleven o'clock that night, and I dared not touch them. Pike were not very pretty to look at. We put them in the deep kitchen sink and placed a heavy bread board over the top. I was reading to the children before bedtime when I suddenly heard thumping noises. We ran into the kitchen to find the bread board jumping up and down. The fish were alive and trying to get out. I wanted to scream. We ran around trying to find heavy items to weigh the board down, hoping they would stay there till Ben came home.

Another scary event was a knock on the door late one night. I opened it to find an Indigenous man leaning drunkenly on the door. He said, "Will the minister take me to the reservation?" He could barely stand up, so I quickly told him the minister was two doors away and shut the door. I was told never to open the door late at night again. Evidently if the local Indigenous people were in trouble, they went to the minister. I was happy the RCMP were right opposite us.

• • •

We had been in Cold Lake six months, with no sign of the lake melting or our belongings arriving from England, when an offer came up for another job with better pay. The job was in Fort Nelson, on the Alaska Highway. Fort Nelson had an eight-month winter, even colder than in Cold Lake. I couldn't see that this would be the kind of life we wanted, but the salary was bigger, with an extra grant for living up North. We would have a home there too, so we finally decided to go. A week before we were to leave, Immigration wrote that our box had arrived from England. Hooray!

The ice was finally beginning to crack and melt as we left Cold Lake. Our furniture had gone ahead with a moving company, so we packed into our old Chevy and prayed that she would get us to Fort Nelson. The car was always plugged into the heater, but at times it still wouldn't start. I wondered how the pioneers ever got anywhere without roads.

The trip to Fort Nelson was 750 miles, so we took turns driving. There was snow, along with sunshine. We were warned to keep our gas tank full, as it could be fifty or sixty miles between stations. Our first stop was Dawson Creek, a.k.a. Mile Zero, a small town at the very beginning of the Alaska Highway, which was 1,500 miles long and gravel all the way.

We drove through canyons, treacherous at times, while I held my breath and wanted to scream. I kept telling Ben there was only about ten inches or less to the edge, but he had the same on his side, so that didn't help. At least the children slept a lot. Our next stop was Fort St. John. It was similar to Dawson Creek, with its lovely little shops. I hoped Fort Nelson would be the same.

We had about a hundred miles left to go when suddenly a family restaurant came into view on the edge of the road. There was nothing else around, so we went in for a meal. Halfway through, the manager came out to tell us a snow storm was heading for Fort Nelson. He advised us to stay overnight, as it could be very dangerous.

The building at the back looked a bit tatty to us. The bed linen was clean, but the room was very chilly. A strong draught was coming from somewhere. We checked the bathroom and found the window was covered with sacking; underneath the sacking was a big hole. Ben went back into the restaurant to change the room or get our money back. The manager refused. I guess that was why they had asked for payment up front. It was so cold, we all ended up in the same bed to keep warm. The wind howled all through the night. In the morning it was too cold to shower, so we had what we called "a lick and a promise," a quick wash. We had a good breakfast, but there was no sign of the manager.

It didn't seem long before we reached Fort Nelson. I had hoped for paved streets, but no such luck. With three motels and a small Hudson's Bay Company store, it reminded me of the old movies I'd seen with Nelson Eddy as a Mountie. I was expecting to see animal furs hanging in the doorways, but that came later. Across the wide roads were small wooden buildings, one a pharmacy, another a movie house. Like in an old cowboy movie, that was all there was. At least in Cold Lake I had been able to drive eight miles to another town. We would have to drive at least 400 miles back to reach a town now, or another 300 miles to the end of the Alaska Highway. I felt we had arrived at the end of the earth.

We had decided to stay at a motel till the furniture arrived. As we took our coats off on the first day, there was a loud knocking on the door. It was a tall heavy man with glasses, who said, "Eee luv, have come to welcome thee."

"Halifax," I said, remembering the accent from the war years when we had visited my cousins. The man had come to show us our new home and hand over the car. Our house was identical to the one in Cold Lake, though the walls were a bit darker. It was up on a hill, with the school next door. At the other end of the town was a small hospital, with two English doctors. The First Nations tribe was different from the one in Cold Lake. I thought it was wonderful how in Canada the different races seemed to get along with each other.

The Hudson's Bay Company store sold everything from clothes to sugar. The food end had lettuce that looked as if it was three weeks old. Mail and newspapers came in only occasionally by air, so we couldn't keep up to date with the news. There was only radio. Everything was more expensive in the North, despite the extra allowance. We could order items from a catalogue, but each item was at least a dollar more.

The gas company Ben worked for was just outside the town, and some of the engineers lived there. I met several of the people Ben worked with. What surprised me was that wherever we went, the children were always sent down to the basement to play, out of the way. The women were always together on one side of the room and the men on the other. We were used to everyone mixing together and the children playing around us.

Children rarely went outside, as it was too cold. That winter it was forty-nine below for six weeks solid. Leaving school, the children only had to lose a glove or uncover their faces to risk frostbite. Our children lost all their peaches-and-cream colouring — they were pale and had red rims around their eyes. Still, Andrew and Ann made many friends, and Margaret seemed to be happy at her playschool.

People still tried to get together. Dogsledding or dancing was held just outside the town. It was still forty-nine below during one dance, and every twenty minutes the men went out to run the cars. The women sat with their coats on most of the night. Annoyingly, Ben had always said that I could only dance with him. That night he danced three times with a very pleasant engineer's wife. Between that and the visits to the car, I felt as if I was totally on my own.

I decided to go to the movies every week. And every week it broke down. No one knew which reel it would be, but we knew it would happen. It was fun, though, and we would have our drinks and popcorn while it was being fixed.

When we first arrived, I kept finding a lovely golden retriever on our doorstep. "Go home," I said. "Don't stay in the cold." A neighbour told me it used to live in our house. Apparently when people left town, they dropped off their pets a few hundred miles down the highway. Sometimes the pets came back, as this one had. Unbelievable just how cruel some people could be. We adopted this one, or rather, took him in.

Ben decided to start studying again. After all these years, I thought it was going to be very hard on him, especially as he was doing shift work. Usually I kept the radio on or played records all day – I loved music, and singing was what kept me happy. But I knew Ben wouldn't be able to concentrate on his studying if I was playing music or singing. When he was on nights, I crept around all day while he slept. I was lost without my music.

Finally we began to see a change in the light outside. The children went to school in the dark and to bed in the light. Winter turned into early spring, and we decided to drive to the hot springs 100 miles up the highway. We saw moose over the hedges, so big and fascinating to watch.

Summer arrived, and we dug over the garden to plant our vegetables. Three feet down, it was still ice. We drove out to have a picnic, and the moment we got out of the car we were swarmed by mosquitoes. We needed to keep our faces covered with netting at all times. The girls' ears were always bloody at the back, where the blackflies liked to nibble. Ben had an allergic reaction to the mosquitoes and ended up in the hospital. He was covered head to toe in blisters. Maybe we were nutcases after all, as Joyce and Laurie had said. If our families had seen where we were living, they wouldn't have believed it.

The local pharmacy was run by an Englishman. We had quite a few chats, and one day he asked me to work for him behind the till. Ben wasn't happy about it, but I had nowhere to go and nothing to do. I felt totally on my own. It seemed all I did was knit Barbie clothes. I needed something to do before I went insane. Working certainly improved my life. It was such fun to be with the other girls, and one of my co-workers was from Yorkshire too.

• • •

A new addition came to our household in the form of a grey kitten named Fluffy, who always slept in Ben's slippers. After two months, he disappeared for three days. We were terrified that the wolves might have got him. Suddenly we heard a faint meow, and eventually we found he was on the very top of an evergreen tree.

One day Andrew was looking out the window and spotted a black bear at the house opposite. It was walking around the carport on two legs, looking inside the car. Then it went around the house and looked in all the windows. I rang the neighbour and asked if she knew a bear was at her house. She often had bears break into her storage shed in the bush — she ran a business and kept a fridge full of food there for the workers — and they would smash everything and throw the food around the walls. Here at the house, the bear had probably come to eat the berries. She called the Mounties, and they came and shot it right away. It was sad to see.

We had seen foolish tourists trying to take pictures of bears on the highway. If cubs get separated from their mother and someone gets between them, the mother bear attacks. We had seen the wardens many a time tell visitors not to get out of their trucks near the bears.

We went to Fort St. John to trade in our old green Chevy for a pale blue one with a mesh shield across the front to ward off bugs. It looked like something from the fifties. We had borrowed four hundred dollars and we planned to pay it off early so we would have a good credit rating. We'd never had a credit card, always paying in cash, but we were told we should build up our credit rating if we ever wanted to buy a home in Canada.

While we were shopping, the children suddenly began jumping up and down, shouting, "Grass, grass, grass!" They had come across a three-foot square of brown grass. I wanted to cry when I saw Ben's face. These poor kids had been through far too much. But they never complained about anything. Like us, they just seemed to adapt to whatever faced us. Andrew loved to go out hunting and to watch the dogsled races. But I could see Ben was very homesick at times. We hadn't had a pair of shoes on in eighteen months.

Some people at the plant found out Ben had been a boiler inspector in his last job and suggested he should apply for government work. They also tried to lure him into investing, but we had learned our lesson the hard way on that. When we had first arrived, Ben had invested $300 into a copper mine that never materialized.

After eighteen months in Fort Nelson, a job came up in Golden, a town in southeastern BC near Rogers Pass. Ben flew to Prince George to sit his First Class Engineer exam, and when he came back we decided to go to Golden. There would be more grass there, and I certainly didn't want another frozen winter if we could help it, though I would miss my job and the old movie theatre. And the Northern Lights were absolutely beautiful to watch.

I salute the people who make a life for themselves in northern settlements. As we left Fort Nelson, we saw a giant moose with his head hanging over the bushes. He seemed to be watching us, saying goodbye. As we left, the girl in the drugstore gave me a little note to give to anyone who may be thinking of moving to Fort Nelson:

Welcome to Fort Nelson, land of opportunity
Where mosquitoes are the largest, the no-see-ums are the smallest.
The lights are the highest. The streets are the darkest.
The sidewalks are none.
Where no one's in a hurry but likes the northern stride
When things begin this year, the next it will abide
Where people are the friendliest. None have come to grieve.
Come to Fort Nelson and you'll never want to leave.

There was no doubt that Andrew would always be in love with the cold north and Canada. He spent the trip writing about the country, including this poem, on the way to Golden:

Canada

The mountains are blue. The rivers are green,
From minerals like copper that give them a sheen.
They sparkle and bubble in canyons below,
Swifter than arrows most of them flow.
The land it is rugged. The pioneers know
They work through short summers and long winter snow
The trees they stand tall. They cover the ground
From high on the mountains, to low on the sands.
They are strong and are proud of their wonderful land.
The great lakes they flow in their own majesty.

Their beauty is something the whole world should see.
There are places, so distant. Where no man has been.
There are goats in the mountains. Bears in the woods.
Moose and deer, everything good.
There are wolves in the winter, looking for prey.
At the sight of a polar bear, please stay away.
The Eskimo hunts, like an Indian band.
They are strong and proud of their wonderful land.
The great lakes they flow in their own majesty.
Their beauty is something the whole world should see.

Andrew

The trip to Golden was 1,000 miles. As we travelled through canyons and passed lakes of sparkling green water, I began to see the beauty of Canada. Golden was at Kicking Horse Pass, sixty-eight miles from Radium Hot Springs, at the junction of the Trans-Canada Highway and Highway 95. It was a cozy, green town nestled between two magnificent mountain ranges, the Selkirk and the Rockies. The moment we arrived we all knew we were going to like it there.

Ben started his job right away and we settled down quickly. The girls were happy, and Andrew loved wandering around on his own at the bottom of the mountains. Ben passed his exam, so to celebrate we all went to Radium Hot Springs. For the first time in a long time, we all seemed very content. Golden was the nicest place we had lived since our arrival in Canada.

Not quite two months after we'd arrived, Ben received a letter from the government office inviting him to interview for a job as a boiler inspector in Prince George. He came back saying the job was everything he could want. We went over everything before making the final decision to go. I knew Andrew would miss Golden, because he'd spent so much time on his own wandering around and loving the little animals. It was a pity we were only there three months.

• • •

The scenery on our trip was beautiful. We went through the Rockies in Alberta – Banff, Jasper and Lake Louise, which was a lovely turquoise. To save money on hotels, we camped, which was a new experience for us all.

I had purchased a sizeable tent, but the stove I had to cook on was quite small. Finally, we arrived in Prince George.

At first we stayed in a first-floor apartment that faced an indoor pool. Wow! The managers were an English couple who had come to Canada on the Queen Mary and toured the country in a Volkswagen camper. They had expected to find a job afterwards, as he was a well-known architect in England with his own company, but it was the old story – he was told he would have to be certified again in Canada. They worked extremely hard, eighteen hours a day, and they needed someone to be in the office to take the rents. They asked me to do it and I agreed. The things I saw! It was unbelievable how some people could live, especially their hygiene.

We took our cat out every day on a leash, but he would not walk anywhere. It was sad to see an outdoor cat being locked up as he was. He would sit looking through the window at the pool, where he could see all the neighbours' animals sitting in their windows. One day he escaped and tore another cat to pieces. He had to be put down immediately. We were so upset. The managers were kind enough to keep him in the office till he was taken away. I will never forget the look on his face as we handed him over. I blamed myself.

We found a nice townhouse. The girls settled in fine, and Andrew joined the Air Cadets. He was a bit of a loner and didn't enjoy sports, so we were pleased for him. Ben seemed to like his job, but I often saw a look of homesickness on his face.

My back had been acting up now and again since Cold Lake. The doctor said it looked like I had been engaged in hard labour all my life. I explained that I had done our laundry by hand for over six months in Cold Lake. He looked at me as if I was mad. He couldn't believe I didn't have a washer and dryer.

Ben had been given a nice big car, so I was able to use the other one as I looked for a job. In all the places we had lived so far, there were no buses. It seemed to me if you didn't drive in Canada, it was like you couldn't read or write. To this day, having been in Canada forty-nine years now, I still have only ever been on one bus.

I was happy to find a job as a cashier in the furniture department of Woodward's on Patricia Boulevard. People loved my accent, and many thought I was Scottish. Even a Scotsman called me "a wee Scottish lassie." I would tell them, "I'm from Yorkshire, a real Yorkshire pudding." People in Canada were from all over the world, and it took time to learn about everyone's different ways. I remember cracking my colleagues up one day when I said someone who'd annoyed me could "stick it up their jumper."

Back came the winter with a vengeance, thirty-nine below again. Prince George was not only cold but also very smelly, with three pulp mills. Still, we did have a lot of fun sliding down the big hill near our home on a tire.

We made it through the winter, but I didn't think I could face another, and I could see Ben felt the same. Did we really want to keep doing this? Nothing we had done so far had made up for the life we'd left behind in England. Maybe it was time to go home again.

Reading a newspaper one day, Ben saw an ad offering cheap airline seats to England. "That's it!" he shouted. "We're off back to England! I'll write a cheque straight away." The girls didn't seem bothered, but Andrew, now thirteen, sobbed his heart out. He wanted to stay in Canada forever, especially up North. Ben was taken aback, but he proceeded to find a chequebook and write out a deposit. A week later, the cheque came back – the seats had been all sold out. My heart sank. Ben said very calmly, "I think someone up there is telling us we have to stay here."

We were disheartened and in a quandary about what we should do. We needed a miracle to happen, and a week later, one did.

On emigration

Growing up in England, in the very heart of the North
We found we had to leave there and set another course.
We moved to lovely Norwich, pretty, peaceful and serene
But always had an urging to fulfill another dream.

Opportunity to travel, perhaps to distant lands
Hardship we were prepared for and to work with willing hands.
With a dream in our hearts, better life for us all,
The decision was made. The going was slow.

The home we'd worked hard for was sold and all gone.
We had made up our minds, so we had to push on.
Well we've travelled a long way and we've all learned a lot.
After three years, was it worth it or not?
All I can tell you, wherever we have been,
My heart's still in England, the land of the green.

Vancouver

On the notice board in his office, Ben spotted a job opening in the city we had always wanted to live in, Vancouver!

He applied for the job right away, but it became very obvious his bosses wanted him to remain where he was. They did everything possible to get him to stay, finally refusing to pay for his transfer. Ben showed them his contract, which stated that any future moves would be compensated. At least three people came forward to say they'd had their first moves paid for. We were new to the country and they had taken advantage of us.

But after some inspectors from the union came by, they soon decided to pay our way.

Vancouver was rainy but beautiful. The winters were milder than anything we had seen so far, but there was plenty of snow on the nearby mountaintops. There was so much to see — parks, museums. It was the first time we had seen whales, porpoises and sea lions.

Even in those days it was far too expensive to buy a home in the city itself. A colleague of Ben's told him about some new houses in Delta, an outlying area. We liked what we saw there — the homes were a reasonable price, the stores and schools were within walking distance, and the large shopping malls were a ten-minute drive away. Everything we needed.

We chose a house with a creek running through the garden. The only mistake we made was paying the full asking price — typical of the English. It never occurred to us that we could make an offer on a new house. Needless to say, nobody mentioned it until after we'd moved in. We were to learn a lot in Canada to shake us out of our shyness.

We told the children they could now have any pet they wanted. Andrew remembered Sooty, the dog we'd had in Norwich, and decided he wanted a dog again. The children knew several friends around us who had to find homes for both kittens and puppies. Soon Andrew came home with a little white and brown springer spaniel. The same day the girls came home with a tiny kitten. Each was six weeks old; I was worried they had been taken away from their mothers too soon. We called the puppy Scamp. The kitten was grey with white markings that looked like buttons, so that became his name. The first night, the puppy was whimpering, and it seemed the kitten wanted to look after him, as it never stopped licking his face. From that day on, they played and slept together. Buttons never meowed. If he saw a rabbit in the garden, he did a little growl, just like Scamp.

We let the children decide whether they wanted to go to the public or the Catholic school, and they decided on the Catholic school. The church wives' club did a lot, arranging the church flowers and fetes, but wives in mixed marriages were not allowed to join. However, they needed someone to drive when the kids' games were at other schools, and to bake cakes for the fetes. The fetes were three-day events to raise money, and the organizers needed cakes for the game with a wheel. They provided the cake mix and asked every family to bake at least one. I usually made half a dozen or more, and the girls and I had fun decorating them.

We worked on the house's basement, building a bedroom for Andrew, a large sitting room, and a laundry room. I loved working in the garden and shaping the creek below. One day I noticed the neighbour opposite looking at me strangely. I had finished doing my jobs inside and had decided to throw a few shovels of soil over the edge of the creek. When I saw her looking at me, I asked if there was anything wrong.

Pulling a face, she said, "I noticed since you moved in you're often cutting the grass, and now you're shovelling dirt. Do you think you should be doing that? After all, it's a man's job."

That, I told her, was a question I had never been asked in my life. My husband had been away for six months at a time for years, so I'd never had a choice. Not only had I had a large garden to look after, but also everything in the home. With two children, one who was often sick, it was full-time work and no one else to do it.

A week later, she was outside cutting her grass. Later on, her friend was out doing it too. Soon we all became good friends. In the winter, when she was scared to drive in the snow, I drove her children with mine.

I regularly corresponded with friends and family back in England. Mum wrote that they wouldn't be able to come over as we'd hoped they might someday. Babs and David got married; we received an invitation but couldn't go. When the photos came and I saw Babs on Dad's arm, it really hit me. Seeing all our relatives laughing together, I sobbed my heart out. I felt lost somehow. I thought how lucky Babs had been to have everybody in the family around her, while I had gone down the aisle with a near-stranger. Not one of my relations had been there with me.

Later, I heard Mum had a lump in her breast and they were going to remove it, and Dad was having trouble with his lungs. The lump, thankfully, turned out to be benign, but Dad had emphysema. It wasn't easy being so far away. I felt helpless.

• • •

I started a night class and began to learn about psychic phenomena. I tried to tell my family about it over supper, a time when we all enjoyed telling stories of our days. I had barely begun when Ben started shaking his head, saying I shouldn't believe in that kind of stuff. This led to a big discussion about the Church, and Andrew wound up agreeing with this father. I told them they could finish their supper without me.

In my hurry to serve dessert, I knocked the dish on the floor. "Why don't you throw some more on the floor?" said Ben. "Maybe you'll feel better." So I did — another three dishes — and I felt good. What a mess! I finished serving dessert and not one of them said a word as they quietly finished their pudding, just looked at me strangely. This was the first time in my life I had thrown dishes, or anything else, in anger, apart from the argument in Norwich. I was getting sick of being told what I should and shouldn't do. I wanted a husband, not a father.

It seemed everything always had to be perfect for Ben. When the children misbehaved, which wasn't very often, he didn't want to know about it. But having everything be perfect is an impossible dream. We have to make mistakes throughout our lives so we can learn by them. Or perhaps it was something else — he always said the children were my responsibility and I was the one who should deal with them and not bother him.

Shortly after this, Mum wrote to say Dad was seriously ill and they didn't think he would survive. Ben said it might be better if I went over to see them by myself. He took out a bank loan and booked my flights for a three-week trip. It had been five years since we'd left England.

I phoned Mum to let her know I was coming, and she told me Dad was in a coma. Apparently everyone was on strike in Hull, and there were no buses or electricity. Barbara would try to go to London for the day and meet me in King's Cross Station. I was looking forward to seeing everybody again, but leaving the children was the hardest thing I had ever done. It was going to be a very long journey.

Back in England

After eleven hours' travel, I finally arrived in London. I missed the bus from the airport by about five minutes and had to wait an hour for the next one. There was nowhere I could get a cup of tea. The streets of London were jammed, and it took over two hours to get to the King's Cross railway station. Luckily, a train to Hull was ready to go — the guard already had his whistle in hand. No sign of Babs. There was only one person waiting, a woman in a black suit with the shortest skirt I had seen in a long time. Her head was covered in a huge red hat and her heels were very high. She looked like a model.

As I was getting my ticket, I suddenly felt someone grab my suitcase. A voice said, "Get your ticket and I'll hold the guard a minute." All I saw was the case going in the door, and I jumped in as the whistle blew. There was the lady in the red hat, with such long eyelashes. It was Barbara! We hugged each other tightly, then spent the next five hours catching up in the dining room. We didn't have time to sleep.

Paragon Station in Hull looked just as I remembered it from the times I had waited there for my dad and Ben. The hospital was well outside the city and the buses were on strike, so we had to take a taxi. It was very late, and I felt stupid carrying my suitcase into the ward. We found Mum sitting by Dad's bedside. He was still in a coma, and they didn't know yet if he was going to come out of it. Mum looked very tired.

By then I had been travelling twenty-eight hours, so we soon went home to sleep. Because of the strikes, residences, hotels and restaurants were allowed to use electricity for only two hours a day. It was obvious Mum had been living on hospital food, and the hospital didn't have a proper cafeteria, only coin-operated machines that served plates of heated food. One day I chose a plate of bacon with one egg — it was like eating a piece of rubber. But the tea was a godsend. The next morning I took Mum to a restaurant downtown and made sure she got a good cooked meal on our way to see Dad.

We talked to Dad for hours, hoping he could hear us. After I had been there three days, he suddenly opened his eyes. We were so happy. "Look who came to see you," Mum said to him. The first words he said to me were "I never thought anything so wonderful could happen to me. I didn't think I would ever see you again." I tried not to cry. Mum was very relieved, and we all decided we would take turns visiting the hospital. Mum certainly needed some rest, as she didn't look well at all.

I was disturbed to learn she had found another lump in her breast, though she reminded me the last one had been benign. I asked her to let me feel it, expecting to find something the size of a small pea. Instead it almost filled the palm of my hand! It felt like holding a hard-boiled egg. When I asked why she hadn't been to a doctor, her excuse — as I'd expected — was that Dad had been sick for a long time and she hadn't wanted to leave him to go into hospital again. I told her if she had gone to the doctor when the lump had first reappeared, it might have proven to be benign again. She promised me she would see her doctor as soon as Dad came home.

Dad got stronger but his breathing remained bad. I guessed his chest trouble was from smoking cigarettes in the Navy — just about everyone I knew who smoked had some kind of chest trouble — and also from working in a chemical plant. I could see he had a lot on his mind.

When I sat and spoke to him alone, he asked me how I felt about the past. I knew what he meant. He said he kept wondering about what I thought and about the trouble over the wedding. I told him it was all in the past and the best thing we could do was to leave it there. He patted my hand and closed his eyes, maybe in relief.

Yes, I had thought about those things over the years, especially when I was on my own. I don't think such things can ever be truly forgotten, though some people do seem to block them out. But, I thought, what good did it do to sit and mope about it? It was all over. The only person I'd told was Joyce, and I knew I could trust her to keep it to herself. I also knew I could never tell Ben — he wouldn't want to know about such things. I intended to put it in the past and get on with my life.

The next time we talked, Dad spoke of splitting the family home between me and Barbara. I told him not to worry about these things and to focus on getting better. Ben had done a good job taking care of us, and he always would. Dad explained that during the war they'd had little to give me, and that it had been much different when Babs was growing up. They'd had a television, sewing machine and typewriter, as well as more money. They wanted to make up for that. I told him Babs had been there when I was thousands of miles away.

After the three weeks were over, I left with a very heavy heart, knowing they all had much more to face. Thank God Babs was there. I carried home with me a large pork pie and a bottle of Tiger Sauce for Ben, lots of chocolate bars from Frank for the children, and our favourite English sweets: pear drops, jelly babies, dolly mixtures and barley sugars. My bag was very heavy.

Ben said the pork pie wasn't quite as he remembered and the Tiger Sauce just tasted like our HP sauce. After all the weight I'd carried! I told him never again.

• • •

After my return Ben and I discussed what to do about future emergencies back home. We decided I would go back to work so we could put aside extra money. I had been thinking about going back to nursing school, but once again it wasn't the right time. It would be easier to get a full-time job without having to study as well, and I had enough to do at home.

I got a position as a cashier in the ladies' department of another store. The people around me were extremely nice, and I loved seeing all the new styles. Most weeks I was able to work six days, and every cent I earned would take us all back to England.

Back home, Dad couldn't walk even a few steps without his oxygen. He had been moved to a bed downstairs. Mum kept her promise to see her doctor. She said she was doing well but didn't reveal any details. Then Babs told us Mum was back in hospital, and I was even more worried than before.

Ben and I had planned to take the children to England next summer, but now we worried summer would be too late. Ben had been saving money also, and we had a good line of credit, so we decided to go at Christmas instead. In addition, Aunt Ivy and Arthur would be getting married, after going out together for sixteen years. Gran had passed away, as had Arthur's mum, and they didn't want to wait any longer. We were so happy for them.

• • •

And so off we went. First we spent a couple of days with Joyce and Laurie and their children in Windsor, and then we went to Hull. The children loved the train ride from London to Hull. They couldn't believe all the greenery in winter. As we reached the Brough area, where we used to live, they saw the giant New Bridge, which went from our side across the water to Lincolnshire. The sad part was now the bridge was built, there were no more ferries.

Dad looked very weak, but he was happy to see us. We knew we had made the right decision in not waiting till summer. Dad had lost a lot of weight and his breathing wasn't good. He had really missed Mum, who was due to come home from hospital in a few days, on Christmas Eve.

Then Barbara brought home some bad news – Mum wouldn't be coming home after all. The nurses had dropped her while trying to get her out of bed, and her leg was broken. She would be in hospital for another three months. I felt so sorry for Dad. Upstairs, the chairs in our rooms were full of Christmas presents Mum had wrapped the last time she was home. It wouldn't be the same without her.

The next day we were up early to go see her. After we had stood at the bus stop for at least fifteen minutes, a little old lady carrying her shopping bag stopped and said, "Eeh, luv, are you waiting for a bus? They went on strike early this morning." We had to find a telephone and call a taxi. The buses, the electricity and even the trains were all on strike. What the heck was happening to this country?

Mum looked well, much better than we had expected, laughing and chatting away with the kids. How much they had grown in six years! she said. When we asked about her leg, she blamed the nurses. I was a bit suspicious about that. While she was talking, Ben went to the ward Sister's office. In the taxi on the way home, he told me what she'd said.

Mum not only had breast cancer but bone cancer too, and she was terminal. This was why her leg had broken after such a short fall – it was so fragile. My biggest shock was that the first lump in her breast had not been benign. I was stunned. Mum had put off checking the lump because Dad was so ill. All she'd cared about was him, and she had let herself go. She hadn't told Aunty Ivy or any relatives that she had cancer. I guess they'd assumed it was the asthma she'd had all her life. The Sister said Mum hadn't seemed to accept it, that she didn't want to discuss it even though she knew she didn't have long to live. I cried hard in the taxi, and then we had to explain it all to the children.

Dad didn't know about all this. Later Babs told me he heard his neighbours discussing Mum in the garden, and that was how he found out she had cancer. How terrible for him to find out that way. I was heartbroken. Now they were both dying, but we didn't know who would go first. I felt so bad for Barbara and David, as they had all the responsibility of looking after them. I knew it wouldn't be possible for me to come back home for a long time.

Christmas was very quiet. We visited Frank at Dianne and Peter's, and he took us to see Ben's mum, "little Grandma" as we called her; my mum was "big Grandma" because she was taller. Then came Ivy and Arthur's wedding.

First we had to have a hen party, which I had never been to before. It was at a German or Swiss pub, like an Oktoberfest. The tables were huge, with long wooden seats, and the beer was poured into huge glasses. Everyone began to walk up and down the tables, singing and dancing. The beer splashed everywhere and we kept getting soaked, but nobody seemed to mind. They just kept dancing and singing together. It reminded me of the beer gardens in Denmark Ben had told me about.

We got home just after midnight, and Ben was waiting at the door. He was furious. Where had we found the nerve to come in at that hour? he wanted to know.

Babs was bewildered, and I wondered if I was hearing right. "It was Aunt Ivy's hen night," I explained. "You didn't expect me to come home early, did you?"

"These children are your responsibility," he said, "and you should set a good example."

Babs gave him a dirty look and left with David. I gave Ben a piece of my mind: "This is the first time in my life that I've been anywhere to have this kind of fun. I'm not drunk. The children went to bed early, or have they been naughty tonight?" The answer of course was no. "It's a good job, then, I didn't come home in the same state you did when Joe had his bachelor party. Frank and Peter had to carry you in!"

I remembered how Mum and Dad used to wait behind the door if I was five minutes late from the bus. It wasn't nice to feel that way again, especially in front of Barbara and David. I went to bed and no more was said. The next day Ben told me he would be going to see his mum at her old folks' home every day. I told him Mum's hospital visits and the wedding would be my priority. I could see he didn't like me answering him back.

The wedding turned out very well, and I was able to see all the relatives I had missed so much. Iris and her mum were there. I had not seen Aunt Olive for years, and this was the very first time I had met Dennis, Iris's husband, and their children. Nobody had met Ben and our children before.

Babs and I sat next to each other at the head table. As we were about to toast the bride and groom, Babs said, "You know this is the end for Mum?" I almost choked. It might have been the wrong time for her to say it, but I knew it had to be on her mind constantly. We needed to be together and talk, but our trip was over before we found the time.

Saying our goodbyes was heartbreaking, knowing it would be a miracle if we ever saw Mum and Dad again. We all parted with heavy hearts. The strikes had gotten worse — trains ran only twice a day, and people had to shop by candlelight. There were rumours that the airlines were going to strike too. We had to wait a long time for a train to London, and when it did arrive it was packed tight, just like during the war years. There were no seats, so we stood in the corridors for three hours while the children sat on the suitcases. We managed to squeeze down for a cup of tea and a tiny snack, but there was very little to eat. With two hours still to go, the ticket collector came around and told us he had five seats available in first class, and we could take them for twenty-five pounds. We did happily, just to be able to sit down for a couple of hours.

London was dark and dismal. There was no electricity, so nothing was lit up. But our hotel was fine, and in the morning we had a lovely English breakfast. We set off for Westminster Abbey only to find most of it was roped off due to terrorist bomb threats. From the museums to Buckingham Palace, it was all the same. The children were disappointed, so we promised to take them to the Tower of London on our last day. We arrived to find it closed.

What with all the strikes, the electricity, the buses, the trains, and the bomb scares, we'd had enough. Never in my life had I thought I would be in a hurry to leave England, but we all felt the same. We couldn't get back to Canada quickly enough.

A Missed Opportunity

Back home I was very restless, thinking of Mum and Dad, wondering if Dad would be around for his next birthday, February 13. His lucky number, he used to say.

I found a five-month business course at the vocational school and gave my notice at the store. They offered me jobs in other departments — shoes, toys — but I wasn't in a frame of mind to do anything. I couldn't focus, and my stomach was acting up. I began to get nervous every time the phone rang, waiting for bad news. I didn't know who it would be when it came; all I knew was that it wasn't far off.

I was sitting at the kitchen table when the phone rang. There was nobody on the other end, just a noise like rushing water, which I had come to know as the overseas sound. I held my breath. No one spoke, so I hung up. Five minutes later I jumped when it rang again. I heard David's voice saying, "Pat, I have some bad news for you."

"Which one is it, David?" I said.

It was Dad. He had died early that morning. I was numb.

Dad was cremated and his ashes taken out to sea at Portsmouth in a naval boat, as he had wished. It must have been terrible for Mum, not being able to say goodbye or go to his funeral. It was impossible for me to go back again. I always regretted that I wasn't able to be there with them.

One day when I was eating lunch, I began to cough and choke. I looked down and found my serviette was full of blood. My doctor arranged for me to see a specialist, and it turned out I had a hiatus hernia. He said it was possible to live with it for a while before surgery.

Six weeks after Dad died, I received a letter from a solicitor in England. It was a copy of Mum's will. It seemed now Dad was gone, she was also ready to go. She had finally accepted the facts. We kept in touch every week, and she sent us a picture of herself in the hospital, sitting up on her pillow with a smiling face and bright twinkling eyes. It looked as if she wanted us to laugh when we saw it and think she was just having her afternoon rest. That was her final picture. Four months after Dad died, we got the sad news. There was no way I could go back — we were still paying off the loan we'd had to borrow for going at Christmas. It broke my heart. Mum was cremated and her ashes were scattered in the rose garden.

• • •

Babs and David decided they needed a holiday after all they had gone through, and I asked if there was any way they could come visit us in Canada. They said they'd see if they could afford it after Mum and Dad's house was sold. In the meantime, for some reason I had an urge to knit baby booties. It was like the urge I'd had years before, when I had a terrible craving for a baby. My thought at the time was that I must give them to Babs, who had been married seven years with no sign of children. I hoped the booties might bring them some luck.

The sale went through and Babs and David finally came to visit. They were fascinated by the differences between our homes. Ours were built with wood, while in England it was brick. Most of our homes had basements, so to them we all lived upstairs. Our electricity was different from theirs, and they kept telling us our light switches were upside down. They wondered why our appliances were so big — though when we visited them a few years later, their fridge was the same size as ours. When we had lived in England we'd been lucky just to own a fridge, and it had only been as big as our dishwasher.

We took them camping, to Banff and Jasper and then on to Lake Louise. They saw all the animals, including some we had never seen — bears, deer, moose. We lunched up in the mountains with the goats walking around our table. I'm sure Mum and Dad were looking down on us. Just before they left, Barbara said she had put on a lot of weight while they were here.

A week or so later, Babs rang me. She had been to the doctor and was over two months pregnant. I had hoped the little pair of booties would bring them luck, but obviously she had been expecting for a while. Something or someone up there must have given me the urge to knit them. I just knew, somehow, there had to be a baby.

• • •

Andrew got a part-time job at a White Spot restaurant so he could pay for his driver's license and buy his own clothes. It was new for us to have children working before they finished school, but it was a common thing in Canada. Most children here left home early and had their own apartments. In England they didn't usually leave home till they married.

Andrew and Ann had both chosen to transfer from Catholic school to public school. Margaret had stayed in Catholic school, but she didn't seem happy there. The nuns didn't like her speaking up for the other girls. They kept comparing her behaviour to her sister's.

Before he had moved to the other school, Andrew had brought home some brochures regarding abortion. The church invited all the families to see a documentary in the church hall, which showed what happened when someone had an abortion. The documentary and the brochures were gruesome to see — enough to scare anyone. After this, Margaret's class was asked to write an essay on the subject. Margaret wrote that it would be better to use birth control to avoid getting pregnant in the first place. Her essay was passed to the head nun, who immediately sent her home for three days. Ben and I went and begged the Sister to let her come back, but the answer was no. She said Margaret had recently become too outspoken, unlike her sister Ann. So much for forgiveness! I was extremely angry. Once again the Catholic Church went down in my estimation. I made up my mind that when Margaret's term was over, she would not be going back there.

• • •

A few weeks ago I had sent out several applications to various banks, and now I finally received a response. After interviewing at the head office in Vancouver, I was offered a job as a teller at a branch in New Westminster, just a twenty-minute drive from where we lived. The staff there were nice and extremely helpful. It was a good wage — in fact, the best I had ever earned.

After I had been there two months, the manager called me into his office and told me I'd done very well. He mentioned they had a special course for their trainees. They spent five weekdays in a nice hotel downtown, working at the head office during the day and hanging out together after supper to go over what they'd learned. The meals were all paid for and it saved travelling back and forth every day.

Ben was not happy when I told him the news. What was I going to do with the children? he asked. They were my responsibility.

"What?" I said. "Goodness, it's only for five days, and they'll be here with you." Here I was with an opportunity to be fully trained, and he was telling me about my responsibility for the children. Now that he was at home all the time, he was equally responsible, in my eyes.

Ben thought about it and said he would bring the children to me in Vancouver every night. What! Had he asked Andrew if he would be at work, or the girls if they wanted to drive an hour there and back for five nights in a row? It was a school week and they went to bed early as a rule. Surely he wasn't going to embarrass me like that. He said if I wanted to go, that was how it was going to be.

I had been changing, speaking out a little bit more, but I was still too shy to face embarrassment like that. Imagine, on a special course, my husband turning up with three children. It made me shiver. Didn't he trust me? Was that why he didn't want me to dance with anybody else? I'd had enough of it, and I stormed out of the room.

I woke up still mad. I knew very well that once Ben had made up his mind he wouldn't change. I sat down and gave my notice. "Due to some family matters," I wrote to my manager, "I will be unable to take the training. Therefore, I have decided it will be best if I don't return to work." Ben would be happy now — he had always liked me being at home. Now he had his wish once again.

I was choked. The best opportunity I had ever had, good pay with good prospects! I had done it with my nursing and now I was doing it again. I had thrown the best opportunities of my life away. What was wrong with me? It seemed to be the story of my life, and it had to stop. I couldn't go on like this or I would never have a life of my own.

As far as I remember, we never discussed the situation again. I adapted to being a mum at home, which had never been hard for me to do. I made up my mind to take more night courses, and this time I intended to do something I liked, without really studying. I decided to do astrology. It might put the cat among the pigeons at home, so to speak. Well, tough. Whenever I went to class, Ben had a sulky attitude. It seemed as if he was punishing me in some way for not working on the house.

Astrology was very different. The teacher read our charts for us, and it amazed me. She told me so much about my growing up, I couldn't believe it. I hadn't told her a thing about myself save my birthday. Still, I never got the hang of reading the charts, even though I learned to make them. My next choice was to learn about past lives. The world is full of things we don't understand — maybe we will only when we go to the other side.

• • •

Our next news was very bad. Scamp had had a large lump removed from his paw twice, and the third time it was cancerous. We could put him to sleep or have his leg amputated. If we did the latter, we would have ten weeks of changing the dressings five times a day. It would be hard work, but the vet thought he had a real chance to recover. We discussed it all together and I told them I was willing to do all the dressings. They decided they wanted to keep him no matter what. Three days before the operation, I was taking him for a check-up. As I cuddled him, I found a large lump in his chest. The vet said they would X-ray it when he was asleep.

We all said our goodbyes the morning of his operation. I took him to the vet and then came home to wait for the results. An hour later the phone rang. It was the vet. While Scamp was asleep, they had X-rayed him and found his lungs and his body were riddled with cancer and he would only last a week or two. I was heartbroken, but what could I do but take their advice? I called Ben at work, something I rarely did. I heard him burst into tears. He came home straight away so we could tell the children together. We were all devastated. As for Buttons, when Scamp didn't come back, he was so sad he stopped eating.

Our last hope was to buy a kitten at the pet shop to keep him company. It was a tiny fluffy ginger boy, and when Buttons saw him he kept growling at him. Then suddenly it was as if he realized this little one needed looking after. He slowly began to come around, and they became very playful together. However, he never did meow, just growled like Scamp. We called this one Fluffy, after the kitten we lost in Fort Nelson. Though, as time went by, it seemed we should have named him Mischief. It was the story of his life.

When I was in the garden, he would dart from our door across the street to our friends' door. He didn't seem to care at all about traffic. I told him that he would do that once too often. He could open any cupboard door. I would find all the doors open in the bathrooms and there he would be, sleeping on the towels. In the kitchen, if we happened to go out, the cupboard was open under the sink when we got back. The bag of crunches would be ripped open. If it was in a cardboard box, he would tip it up on its side. If he was hungry, he always helped himself. We were really surprised at what he could do.

One day Ben was putting a new unit together with sliding doors, and Fluffy was sitting beside Ben, watching what he was doing. Ben told him that he wouldn't be able to open these doors. Ten minutes after it was put together, there he was, tapping it with his paw, and the door came sliding open. That's how clever he was.

As we were coping with the loss of Scamp, strangely enough, another springer spaniel came on our driveway. He was chocolate brown. The children were playing, and he seemed to want to be with them. He had no identity disc, and at the end of the day he wouldn't leave them.

Margaret asked us to keep him. I said no at first, but three days later he was still with us and nobody was asking about him despite the notices we had placed throughout the neighbourhood. Margaret cried her eyes out when we took him to the pound, saying they would put him down. Needless to say, he became the next member of the family.

He was Mischief number two. If we went out, he had the run of the garden. Every time we came back, everything would be buried three feet deep — shoes, boots or tools, anything he could carry. This went on for months. No wonder no one came looking for him. He was a Dennis the Menace, but so lovable. We named him Shane.

One day while I was home sewing, my chiropractor called and asked if I could come work for him. Somehow he had learned I had left the bank. He offered to pay me slightly more than I had earned as a cashier. Ben said it was my decision, provided it didn't interfere with the household routine.

I had heard that a bit too often over the years. It seemed that nothing was to be disturbed, especially him. I felt I had never been number one in our lives. I never doubted he loved me; it was just that maybe he loved himself just that little bit more. He never wanted to be put out, so really he was number one, even before the children. Everything he had ever wanted he'd got, like moving to Canada. Well, here I was thinking things that in England would never have crossed my mind. This proved how much I had changed.

It was another opportunity to work, so I went ahead and took the job. Little did I know it was going to change my life. It was an extremely busy office. I worked there three days a week, and the chiropractor's wife worked the other two days. I loved meeting the people, but my boss seemed to have a lot on his mind and I often noticed him looking a bit depressed.

When we moved to new offices, I offered to paper the walls using the nice modern wallpaper his wife had picked out. It turned out so well, she asked me to do the kitchen too. As a thank-you, they took Ben and me out to dinner. It happened to be our twenty-third wedding anniversary; we had never been out to celebrate one before.

I was surprised when my boss asked me a question about astrology. He wanted to know how two people with birthdays three days apart could be so different, one so warm-hearted, the other very cold. I explained that people born even a minute apart can be total opposites, depending on the planets and several things in their charts. Jokingly, I told him I was a Gemini, the sign of the twins, and that Geminis were often two different people at any time.

I guess many of his patients really confided in him. He said he couldn't believe how many long-term marriages seemed to be falling apart. He reminded me of our old English doctors, always worrying about his patients, on call for anyone who needed him. It was wonderful to see someone who really cared about people.

At work lunchtime often ran late, so instead of rushing home we usually made a quick snack. I was walking through the kitchen door to say lunch was ready, when my boss walked right into me. His arms went around me and he kissed me passionately.

Blown Away

I stood there and stared back at him, not saying a word. I think I was too startled to say or do anything.

His face turned very red. He later told me that he was glad I hadn't pushed him away and been angry with him. All I could do was ask if there was something wrong, because I had noticed how depressed he seemed at times.

My boss, who I will call Kevin, had been married thirty-two years. Once the children were grown, he just wasn't happy. Many times he had thought about leaving the relationship, but he worried about what people might think. Long before I came to work for him, he confided, he had been attracted to me. He had wanted to hold me for a long time but had felt guilty, knowing what a lovely family we were.

Had I done anything to encourage this situation? I hadn't had a clue he felt like this. I was sure of one thing — I loved my job and my co-workers. I admired so much the way he treated people. When he'd actually kissed me, how had I felt? My goodness! Was I suddenly aware of a passion between us?

Ben had been acting more like my dad again. Could that be why Kevin and I talked so much? Was it easier to talk to each other than our spouses? I was always on guard about what I said to Ben because I didn't want to upset him. He was probably hurt by my speaking out more, choosing to go to night school, and mixing with people. He just wanted me to be the same person I had been when we fell in love. Through all we had experienced together, I had never stopped loving him, but he wasn't changing. Maybe that was our problem.

I wanted to be with my family — they were my life. Ben booked us a seven-day bus trip to Reno, our first time going somewhere without the children. He had decided they were old enough now to look after each other, and I had to promise not to worry about them. Easier said than done. Before I left work, Kevin gave me a long hug and a tiny silver St. Christopher medal, to bring me safely back to him, he said.

The trip went well, but when we got back my stomach felt heavy, as if everything I had eaten was still sitting there. I went to my doctor, who told me to go straight to the hospital. If I improved after two days, they would send me home. If not, they would operate. Two days later, I was being prepped for surgery. They told me they would repair my hiatus hernia and check my stomach as they opened me up for a suspected ulcer.

I woke up with tubes everywhere. Half-asleep, I asked my doctor if I had cancer, or had they removed my stomach? He told me that, in addition to the hernia, I had a duodenal ulcer in the entrance of my stomach and the whole inside of my stomach was scarred end to end. I must have had chronic ulcers all my life.

They did something they didn't often do to people so young — gave me a vagotomy, the cutting of the vagus nerve to reduce acid flow. This nerve controls many things in the body, as I would later find out. After eleven days they removed some of my tubes and I was allowed to walk around pushing a drip. My throat was terribly sore and all I could swallow were liquids and Jell-O. Kevin came to see me during his lunch hour, saying how much he missed me and loved me with all his heart. Bidding adieu was an excuse to kiss me again. I watched him walk down the corridor, and suddenly I wanted to run after him and hold him tight.

After three weeks' rest at home, I went back to work. I couldn't wait to see him, and we fell into each other's arms. I think we both realized then how we felt about each other. I knew it was very wrong and that there would be consequences, but I also knew I had fallen deeply in love. Kevin kept talking about us going away and setting up a new business. What would people, or my children, think?

My relationship with Kevin never seemed like an affair. There was no going out together in the evenings or spending weekends together. Occasionally we went for a walk in the park at lunchtime. Twice he greeted me at night school while my classmates were around, and afterwards we managed to sit in his car and talk for ten or fifteen minutes. We wanted so much to be together all the time, but it wasn't possible. It would have to be the right time, and we would have to face everyone together.

• • •

Three months after my surgery, I still didn't feel quite right. A few times I passed out after climbing the stairs at home. I had never been a person for fainting. Tests showed my stomach was not absorbing iron, and I now had pernicious anemia. I began injections of B12 daily for a week, then weekly for a month. I was lucky — in another era this disease could have been a death sentence. Now there were regular injections every month for the rest of my life. I would be fine.

After the vagotomy I began to have problems throughout my body — inflammation from my pancreas through my bowels and into my bladder. I was sent to Vancouver General Hospital for five days. Diarrhea began to be a problem. I had been told it might occur for the first year after my surgery, but unfortunately it became chronic, something I would have to deal with for the rest of my life.

Ben arranged a week's holiday in Hawaii, something I'd always dreamed of. I thought it was the most beautiful place in the world. I felt so rested by the end. I could have stayed there forever.

Andrew, now almost twenty, was ready to go work in the bush. He had found a job at an engineering company to learn surveying, starting off in Whistler. Now he was beginning a life in the cold North, an isolated and lonely life that he himself had chosen. A year later, I still set the table for five out of habit. When he wasn't there at Christmastime, even if he phoned us, I cried my eyes out, thinking he was alone without his family. Ann graduated from school and prepared to leave home. She began work in a bank downtown, sharing a place in Vancouver with a friend who was in nursing school. Another one had left the nest.

I began a new night course on how to read auras. One night an instructor, Gloria, put her hand on my shoulder and asked if I would stand for her. Laughing, she said I was completely surrounded by yellow, so I must be the biggest softie going. It was true — so many people in my life had taken advantage of me. Still laughing, she said, "For a minute you had a halo, and then it fell from your head down to your shoulder. You looked like a fallen angel." Then she said something had happened to me at the end of October. Something that, though I might not realize it yet, was going to change my life forever. I held my breath. It had been the end of October when things had started with Kevin. I was scared. We had been taught as children that we would have to pay the consequences for what we did.

Kevin had been to our house, and the children liked him a lot. Sometimes he brought his wife over, even after we had gone out to dinner. If he'd stopped bringing her over, both she and Ben would have wondered why. A woman in my class who said she knew Kevin dropped some hints that he might have had an affair with someone else. Sitting outside in the garden one lunchtime, I asked if he had met someone else after his marriage started failing. He admitted he had liked someone but her husband had begun to get a bit nasty. The husband went to see him and Kevin told him, "It takes two."

"If Ben knocked on your door and accused you, would you say that to him too?"

His face went a little red, but at that point his wife walked into the garden, so I didn't get my answer. He began to talk more about us moving away together and starting a new business.

That weekend I had a dream. I was in his house, which was very modern. I went upstairs, searching for him. From the balcony I looked down into the sitting room. I could hear him and his wife arguing in a bedroom. She came out in a rage and went down the stairs. Through the bedroom door, I saw a large bed with a blue duvet with huge white flowers on it. Kevin got into bed and went to sleep. I kissed him on the head, and then I was home again.

One evening I received a phone call from his wife, who said he was seriously ill in the hospital. He'd had a very bad stomach hemorrhage, during which he'd lost so much blood he'd almost died. It had taken several transfusions to bring him back. She asked if I could take care of the office. I was deeply worried but, being in the office all the time, I couldn't go to see him. When he was allowed visitors I popped in, but there were too many people there and we couldn't speak on our own. He said he would be going home the next week and to come over with Ben at the weekend. He really looked terrible. The room had emptied, so I was able to give him a quick kiss before I left.

That weekend we went to their house. It looked very modern, designed by a well-known architect. His wife offered to show me around the house while the tea was brewing. I climbed the stairs as if I had done it before, though I had never been there until now. From the balcony, I looked down into the sitting room where Kevin and Ben were chatting away. When we went into the bedroom, I had to hold my breath. There on the bed was a blue duvet with large white flowers, just as I had seen in my dream. Everything was identical. I was positive I had been there before, somehow, in my dream. I reminded myself to ask my teacher Gloria about out-of-body experiences.

Kevin got better and was soon back at work. It was strange that we had both ended up in hospital. I was sure it was because of all the guilt and worry. We had brought it on ourselves and now we had to deal with it. Kevin's reputation was always his worry, but he told me repeatedly he never wanted me to leave him. It was on my mind so much that I had a big nightmare.

In the dream, he told me to pack my bags and meet him at dawn outside the office. We would leave no matter what. We could go anywhere together. I left at midnight and sat in the car for hours, looking at the early morning fog. I knew in my heart his reputation would stop him coming in the end. I woke up and felt my heart breaking. No matter how much he loved me, it couldn't happen. To me, this was another warning.

I told Kevin about my dream. He held me tight and said, "This has to work for us. We can do anything together. I'll never let you go." What could I do?

• • •

Aunt Ivy rang to say she would like to come over for a visit, and Andrew promised he would come home to see her. We did our usual trips to Alberta and she loved it. We took her to the beach in Penticton; she hadn't worn a bathing suit in over forty years. She sunbathed and ate ice cream and was, as we say, absolutely tickled pink.

When we got home, we introduced her to Kevin and his wife, and we all went to dinner. Aunt Ivy thought he was a super person and was really smitten with him. I wondered how she would feel if she knew about us. I was a bit scared, because Kevin kept trying to hold my hand under the table. I had never seen his wife laugh so much.

The girls brought some of their friends over, and it was comical to see the look on Aunt Ivy's face. One was Black, another Indigenous, the other two white. Her eyes never left them and she was extremely quiet. I realized she would never have seen such a mixture of people socializing like this – certainly not in England when we were growing up. One evening we introduced her to another friend, Randy, who was Black. She seemed a bit flustered, never saying his name all night. I asked her if there was anything wrong, and she explained she was scared to repeat his name because in England it had a very different meaning, and it was embarrassing to say it out loud.

Aunt Ivy went back home and Andrew returned to the North. Some time later, Barbara had her third baby. The first two were girls, the image of our mum and dad. Rebecca, the eldest, had been born two hours before my dad's birthday. Seeing her, it was as if his eyes were staring out at me. The second, Rachael, was like Mum, and reincarnation came to mind. Maybe they were going to be together again in a different way. When the third one was born, it was another girl, Roberta. She was very much like David.

I decided I had to talk to my friend Gloria, the psychic. She explained that, in another time and place, Kevin and I could have been soul mates. In this life, our love was very real, but due to karma from Kevin's previous lives, he had much to learn before it could happen. At this time, it was not meant to be. In my heart I knew she was right. I don't remember ever being as sad as I was then, racked with guilt and a terrible shame. I had to leave; it was best for everyone. Yet I knew someday I would tell Ben what I had done.

Time to Say Goodbye

It seemed like a good time to go back to nursing. I had applied to college and been accepted, and now I had to tell Kevin and give my notice. I decided to drop a hint. I remarked that, as Margaret was grown up, it might be nice to start my nursing again.

I will never forget the look on Kevin's face. "You would never leave me," he said.

"It might be the answer for both of us," I said. I didn't want either of us to end up back in hospital. What if his wife and Ben found out about us? He said very little after that, but I got lots of hugs and he held me very tightly.

I gave him a month's notice. I didn't think I would ever stop loving him, but I just couldn't go on this way. I had worked for him for three years now, and I couldn't live with myself anymore. He was in tears when I left him that night. For the next month, I think he believed I would change my mind. When I saw how many times he wept, I wondered if I would be able to walk out. The final goodbye was heartbreaking for both of us. He was sitting at his desk with his head down. I knew he was devastated. I returned my St. Christopher medal and some little souvenirs he had bought me over the years. I had to force myself to walk out the door for the last time.

It took every bit of strength I had not to call him the first three weeks after we ended our relationship. He was always on my mind. My head kept playing the song I loved by Barbra Streisand, "He Touched Me." My only answer was to keep myself extremely busy.

Six months passed and I didn't hear anything. Then one day I was walking to my car and heard someone say "Hello, Pat." It was his wife, with a very stern face, just staring at me as she walked by. I was so glad she didn't stop. She didn't look too happy, though she never was one to smile much. Two weeks later, I bumped into someone who knew them both. She'd heard Kevin had left his wife and was living on his own. No wonder his wife hadn't looked happy! He was finally free. I wondered if she knew about us. Only time would tell if I would hear from him again. Either way, my leaving had somehow triggered his decision to look to his future. I hoped for him it was the right one.

• • •

I had failed one subject, Pharmacology, and the college wouldn't let me continue into the next year without it. I applied for a job as a nurse aide at Burnaby General Hospital and was very lucky to be taken on for a permanent part-time job in Extended Care. I loved working with elderly people. I was able to work and also retake the college Pharmacology course.

When a nurse on the ward below left to have a baby, I was offered her position for six months. In the end, she didn't come back, and it turned into a full year. The shift-work hours were long and the salaries very low. We worked six days on and two off, with one weekend off in five weeks.

I made friends with a Filipina woman named Remy, who was married with two sons, and with another woman named Wendy. As soon as I heard Wendy speak I said, "My goodness, that has got to be a Hull accent!" What a small world. We had lived a short distance from each other back in England, and she had also worked in Bournemouth, very near to Joyce. From that day on, Wendy, Remy and I were life-long friends.

• • •

Around Christmastime, Ben, Margaret and I went to church as usual. When communion came around, the young priest said very abruptly, "I don't want to see any non-Catholics from the mixed marriages taking communion tonight. We're far too busy." This had never even occurred to me, and the nasty way he said it made tears run down my cheeks. Ben grabbed my hand, and neither he nor Margaret took their communion that night. I felt like walking out and never going back. I made up my mind that from then on they could go to church without me. I would talk to God on my own. I didn't need a church for that.

Ben wanted me around all the time, but I needed some space. He loved to work around the house, changing things and working on the cars. He also liked to paint as a hobby and was very good at it. Yet if I went to night school and made any friends, he'd sulk. I couldn't breathe, and I felt we were becoming different people. We had more arguments than normal, which began to upset Margaret. She told us she wanted to quit school and go to work. We weren't happy about it, but she had never really settled in at school.

One day I bumped into an old friend who told me Kevin was living with a woman who worked in a bank. I was hurt that he'd never tried to get in touch with me, but in a way I was glad he hadn't. I had wondered how it would be if we met again now that he was free, and now I had my answer. It didn't stop me from being in love with him.

I went into my second year at college, though I still managed to work on weekends. I did my Maternity unit in a hospital named Grace. It was wonderful. We saw two births and learned so much.

Some days Ben seemed so possessive that I felt I had to get away. Finally the day came when I told him I needed to be on my own for a while. Needless to say, he was extremely upset. I had loved him for many years, and I had never wanted to hurt him. He'd looked after us so well and we had a lovely home — but I felt he didn't like me as I was now. I wasn't the person he'd brought to Canada. He was someone who would never hurt anyone deliberately, but I felt he was trying hard to control me. I don't think he realized what he was doing.

He asked me what was going on. I said I just wanted some space. We were arguing too much. Then I had to tell him about my affair with Kevin. I couldn't live with my guilt any longer.

It took a while. When I was done, he got ready to go on his nightly run to think about it, but I said there was one more thing I had to tell him first — when I was a young girl, my dad had sexually abused me. His face went as white as the tablecloth, and he went out the door without a word.

It was almost three hours before he came back. He sat down at the table, ready to talk. I made some tea and sat down. First he wanted to know if I was going to leave him for Kevin. I said no, I just wanted my own space for a while. He said no matter what had happened, he never wanted me to leave him.

While I was trying to be honest about everything, a question popped into my head — had he ever been unfaithful? He looked straight at me and said, "Yes, I was. I came off the ship with a group and we went to a beer garden for a few drinks. Singing and dancing together, we drank too much. The next morning I woke up in some woman's bed. It happened only once, after we'd been married ten years."

I wondered if he was perhaps forgiving me because he had been feeling guilty himself for a long time. But I think he got it wrong. When we came to Canada we had been married over eleven years, and we were in Norwich for four and a half years. The beer gardens I remembered were on his short trips to Denmark, after we were married and before Andrew was born. When Andrew was born he came ashore for a year, and after that he went on the supertankers to Saudi Arabia. So it must have been during the first three to four years we were married. I was surprised, because those had been very good years. I told him I felt very guilty for what I had done, but it had taken me twenty-four years to go wrong.

He told me when he was at sea he had often wondered if I might meet someone else. I had to laugh. How could he even think that, after all we had been through to get married? How on earth was I likely to meet anybody, being with our children twenty-four hours a day and seeing only two people, his mum and Frank, and now and again a neighbour?

We could look at it from many angles, but I still wanted a break. I told him I was going to stand on my own feet. I wouldn't ask him for anything, just time on my own. Andrew and Ann would be upset, but they were living their own lives — it was Margaret I was most worried about. I just wanted Ben to take care of her for a while. Ann was indeed upset. She said she would come home and stay with her dad and Margaret.

A friend of mine had told me about a bedsitter apartment for rent, quite reasonable, and a few weeks later I decided to take it. I told Ben I wouldn't touch the joint savings. He had more savings than I had, and a top job, so he had nothing to worry about financially, just the mortgage. I had always handled all the bills, and I knew he would be fine. I did hope the break would do us both good. If he really wanted me back, we could try again.

Ben and I seemed to have more arguments in the next three weeks over the phone than we'd had in all the years we'd been married. He said I could still have my monthly pocket money at least, especially as I was in college. I wasn't sure what to do about that, having said I would stand on my own two feet. Whenever he'd given me money before, he always wanted to know what I was spending it on. It shouldn't have mattered, if it was mine. However, in the end all he brought me was a Visa bill for seventy-five dollars that he said was mine.

All I had taken with me from home was a few bits of cutlery and some dishes. I couldn't afford a bed, so Ann offered to lend me hers. Ben said Ann's bed was much too big for my place. He sold it to a neighbour and said he would bring me our sofa bed. I was excited to have more space, but unfortunately in the meantime I had to sleep on the floor in a sleeping bag. It took him six months to bring the couch over.

Finding Happiness
1985 — present

All By Myself

It took me a while to adjust to being on my own and not worrying every single minute about the children, the house, the animals and the meals. I felt guilty for putting myself first, but it was a big sense of freedom – meals when I wanted and no questions when I got home. It was the first time in my life I could do anything I wanted.

By the end of my second year of college, money was evaporating and I knew I wouldn't be able to finish my final quarter. I went to see if I could get some help or a student loan. Well, try getting a student loan when you're married! My only option was to go back to work and return to finish college later. I rang the hospital and they said I could have five-day shifts if I started on Christmas Eve. I was relieved to have work offered to me. At the end of the term I left college, and a week later I was back in my favourite ward.

I loved working in the Extended Care Ward. Some patients were lucky enough to have relatives who visited and helped feed them, but the majority relied on us. Most of us looked upon them as our other family and thus liked working Christmastime and holidays. We all got along well. After the late shift a few of us often had a snack at a nearby café.

Though I had left college, I had finished enough courses to sit the examination to be a practical nurse. In those days, the practical nurses did everything except give medication. I passed my exam with above-average marks and was given a big certificate with my new number, stating I was now a member of the Practical Nurses Association. Though I would receive a better salary, the idea of leaving my second family in Extended Care really shook me.

Ann asked me to her apartment for Christmas Day with Margaret and Ben. Sadly, it didn't go well. Ben hardly spoke a word, and when it came to opening our presents, mine from him wasn't there. Suddenly he said he was leaving. There was no "Merry Christmas" or "Happy New Year," just "Bye." I thought he was very rude to act that way in front of our children. Needless to say, I was the demon for having left in the first place.

• • •

One night after my shift I was invited to go to the local pub for a drink. I thought I should see what single life was like out there and introduced myself to a football team. Quite a few of them were English and Scottish, and they enjoyed playing a game of darts at the pub. They were all very pleasant and nobody laughed when I chose to drink coffee. I did move on to a large 7 Up with a splash of beer, the old English shandy.

Eventually I was asked out to lunch a couple of times by someone from the hospital. He had been divorced for twenty-five years. The more we talked, the more he reminded me of Ben, and I wondered if that was the attraction. I decided not to get involved. Every time I met someone, I said I was planning to go back to my husband. At times I thought things seemed quite sordid out in this world. Once or twice Ben and I went to a movie. I asked him if he wanted a divorce. He said no, and I wasn't in a rush either. I felt we still might want to try again. Time would tell.

One night my group of girlfriends and I saw a great Scottish trio in the pub. My friend S mentioned that her husband was visiting family in England, and when I asked why she hadn't gone with him, as she was English, she said she wanted to spend the time with her boyfriend. They were going to tell her husband about their relationship when he came home. Weeks later, we walked into the pub with our husbands and saw S sitting with a very nice-looking man. She looked miserable. In the washroom, we asked S if she and her boyfriend would like to join our table. "You silly buggers," she said, "that's not my boyfriend, it's my husband."

S's husband, John, seemed a very quiet person, and to my surprise he and Ben chatted all night. They had a lot in common, as both were boiler inspectors in different cities. The entertainment was great and everyone danced with each other, but S didn't ask John to dance. She was off trying to steal a young girl's boyfriend. The girl was getting angry but S didn't seem to care. I felt bad for John, the only one left out of the dancing. He seemed so nice, not at all the ogre he'd been made out to be. Then I did something I had never done before — I asked John to dance. On our way home, Ben couldn't stop saying what a nice chap he was.

A short time later I bumped into John while getting groceries at the mall across the road. He asked me for a coffee and we had a nice chat. He was very easy to talk to. He told me he had decided to move out and had been looking around for a place.

• • •

Ben decided he wanted to sell the house. If I moved to a two-bedroom apartment, he said, Margaret could live with me and he would pay her half the rent. I found a nice one-bedroom with a big den, and Margaret and I moved in together. I signed the papers for Ben to put the house up for sale. He said if it was sold, he would make sure the notary gave us two separate cheques. I was quite pleased that I would finally have some savings and my own car.

When my car insurance came around, I told Ben I would like it to be in my own name. He was very reluctant to do this. He told me in front of the agent that if it was signed over to me, it would be my full responsibility. It was embarrassing being told like that.

One night near midnight I found my car totally frozen in the parking lot. My new BCAA card was still at home, so I rang Ben, who was just seven minutes down the road. He read me the number and went back to sleep. I didn't get home till nearly two o'clock in the morning. I guess that was the responsibility I had to take on once the car belonged to me.

Ben found a buyer for the house and bought another house in Coquitlam, near a new shopping mall. He made it very clear that this house was going to be in his name only, but he said if I liked to do some wallpapering or put bushes or flowers in the garden, I could. The only thing was, I would have to pay for it. When he was settled, he said, we could talk about getting back together. This was a lot to think about. I knew he would need some help to move, and I was happy to help him any way I could. It had always been my intention to go back to him, and I thought if he really wanted me back home, then maybe this time we could make it work.

• • •

One night the phone rang and it was John. He invited me for a coffee and said he had something to tell me. When he arrived, Margaret was the one who answered the door, saying, "Hi, John. Welcome to the morgue." They laughed and hit it off right away.

He had moved into an apartment in Surrey. When I told him I had passed my exams, he said he'd come over and take some pictures of me in my full uniform. The next night, he came with his camera and a lovely bouquet of yellow roses. Ben saw the photos and asked who had taken them. When I told him, he pulled a face and began acting very grumpy, as if he was getting jealous again. I guessed I should have expected that if he wanted me home again, but I knew he had also been seeing someone.

Whenever I had my week of day shifts, John and I saw each other for coffee and the odd supper. I knew he was still struggling to pay rent and support his wife, so we always took turns paying. He had tried several times to settle with his wife, but she refused to sign anything. There was no doubt John and I were very fond of each other. He had become my best friend. We laughed a lot, but I was getting worried about hurting him. He had known about my intention to go back to Ben since the day we met. I told him the best thing we could do would be to stop seeing each other for at least three months. I had to see if this marriage had a chance to work.

We had often done a lot of talking over the phone. Now it was terribly quiet. Occasionally when I called my friends, it was John I ended up speaking to instead. I would swear that I never rang his number, but there he was. I would realize when I heard his voice that I had missed him very much. After that we didn't talk, but he wrote me some letters when he knew I still hadn't gone home.

Before finally going back to Ben, I had to go into the hospital once more. I had endometriosis and polyps, and I had been on the waiting list for a while. My hemoglobin went down to seven, and the doctor said I couldn't go on losing any more blood. Two days later I had a hysterectomy. Two days after that, I had a vein in my in leg stripped. The nurse said I must be a real glutton for punishment. Early the next morning, before visiting time, John walked in carrying a large bunch of yellow roses. My friend had told him I was in there. Ben came in later, with a huge pot of yellow chrysanthemums. He saw the roses and wanted to know where they'd come from. He put on a face when I told him.

While in hospital, I thought I might use my time off to go to England and see my family. It seemed like forever since I had seen Babs, David and the rest. When I told Ben, he said he didn't want me carrying suitcases after my surgery and would like to come with me. I guess I had got used to living on my own — I really wanted to go to England alone.

Ben suggested I come home first before I did anything else. If I was ever to move back in, the time was now. The children, of course, were very happy, and Margaret came with me. Ben and I finally had sex again for the first time in a long time. I was hoping it would be fine after the operation, but I was still a bit nervous, as well as shy. All the years we had been married, we'd had a good sex life. This night I wouldn't want to repeat what he said to me afterwards. I will just say that part of our relationship came to an end, which kind of put a damper on things.

• • •

Ben talked me into going to England with him. First we visited Joyce and Laurie, who had moved to Bournemouth, and then we went to see Babs and David and their three cute girls. They couldn't get over how well I looked after my operations. I think they were expecting to put me in a wheelchair. I jokingly said, "It's all in the head, and I'm staying around till I'm ninety-seven to torment everyone." I still say this today.

Frank took us to the seaside to see their mum, who seemed happy in the home and went down the road every day to her favourite café for her tea and scones. Frank still lived with Dianne and Peter. When we left for Canada, they'd had three big removal vans; now they had nine. Frank also took us to see Joe and Frances in Bridlington and we had a lovely day all together. That was the last time we saw Joe, as he died two years later.

We went to see my friend Mary, whose husband Bill had given me away at my wedding. Bill had passed away and Mary lived on her own, but her sister Sue, who had made sandwiches on our wedding day, still spent time with her. During our visit Ben frowned a few times and I wondered why. Was it because once again I was with a friend? Had I spoken out of turn about something?

We were on the way home when I asked what was wrong. He said I had said things about women and their independence that he didn't like. If I were to come home, he explained, there were going to be a few rules.

I told him there were going to be no rules. It had to be fifty-fifty. Most marriages have give and take at times, but not all the time. I told him if he started again with rules, I would be moving out.

• • •

Back in Canada, I checked the notice board for practical nurses' jobs, but there were none — only a request for a volunteer in the morgue to cover a two-week holiday. When I told Ben I might volunteer, all I got was a dirty look. For three days he hardly spoke a word to me. Here we go again! I thought. What had I done now?

The thought of me handling dead bodies then coming home afterwards really upset him. I tried to explain that even as a student nurse in England I'd had to lay people out. Now with the elderly it was a regular part of our job, and sometimes there were many at once. We took them to the morgue ourselves. When there is a death, you have to look after them and treat them with dignity and respect right to the end. I said to Ben that if I had told him how many people I had laid out over the years, he might not have spoken to me ever again. In the end, a male nurse volunteered to do the morgue job, so he didn't have to worry about it.

I hadn't seen much of my friends since I'd moved back home, so I was happy when B said she would come to my house for a cup of tea. She was delayed, and rang to ask if I could meet her at a nearby store and have a coffee there. This was fine with me, but Ben became angry. He wanted to know what time the store closed and when I would be home again. It seemed he didn't like me to go out.

• • •

Margaret worked very hard and got her driver's license. Andrew was working for an oil company. It was minus sixty-two degrees where he was. Sometimes we had no idea where he was, but we knew it would be in the cold or in the bush. One of these days I was going to have to stop worrying. He was grown up. I honestly think that once a mother, always a mother. The love is there forever, no matter what.

It came to my mind many times that if Ben had come to Canada on his own for the first six months, he would have been back in England after Cold Lake or Fort Nelson. For us it would have been just like another six months of him away at sea. I asked myself if, had we still been in England, we would have split up, or would we still be the same old couple in love? I knew now that things might never be the same again. There was always a reason for everything, we just didn't know it yet.

One night Ben and I went to a movie, and driving home we both were extra quiet. We were listening to soft music on the radio. I felt suddenly lost and totally sad, and the tears flowed down my face. Ben glanced over and gave my hand a quick squeeze. Very quietly he said, "This is the end, isn't it? It's over between us." I didn't say a word or I would have just choked. We both knew the answer.

The Final Move

The next day Ben offered to help me move if I wanted to find my own place. We agreed it was for the best. He said he could move me at the end of the month, my only weekend off. The sad thing was that it was his birthday. I felt so bad. I told him I would take him out to dinner. It was the least I could do. The first time I had moved, I'd only had cutlery and dishes. This time I would take the new furniture I had bought. Ben pulled a face again.

When our house had sold, Ben had given me my half of the money and I'd put it away. I hadn't intend to spend a penny of it. But then he asked if I would lend him some extra money to put on his new mortgage, and I did. When we were trying to decide about getting back together, we went to Las Vegas, twice, at his suggestion. He had asked me to pay for the trips and said he would pay me back half later. The trip to England, too, cost much more than I'd planned — the cheap flight I'd found didn't fit with Ben's schedule so we'd had to book another, plus there were the BritRail passes and a new suitcase for Ben. Our three-week trip cost just over $4,000. I had a bigger shock when Ben asked me to pay for it, saying he'd pay back his share later. He had a top job, so I thought I wouldn't have to wait long. Now he paid me back what he owed me for his mortgage, but there was no discussion about sharing the cost of our three trips.

I was going to need every penny I could save from now on. To buy anything and take out a mortgage, I would need to have a full-time job and at least a 10 percent deposit. I was still working part time, and I could never get a mortgage on my salary. In all the five years I'd lived on my own, I had lived below the poverty line.

I decided to get a credit card of my own. Ours had always been joint, and after many years we had a very good credit line of a few thousand dollars. When I applied, they gave me a card with only a $300 credit limit. Was this how women on their own were treated? I thought of how hard I had worked to look after my family and what opportunities I had given up. I wanted to stand on a rooftop and scream to women out there, "Don't marry until you have a good job and can stand on your own two feet!" After I'd calmed down I realized that if I hadn't married when I did, I wouldn't have had my lovely children. They had often told me how happy they were that I was always at home for them when they finished school. It was my choice now to leave, so I would have to get through it by myself.

I talked to a lawyer about a divorce. Because I had gone back home, I would have to wait longer. He could try, he said, but it would cost me almost $4,000. No way could I afford that, so I would wait out the five years. Now that we were involved with lawyers, it was going to cost me even for minor things. Ben suggested that we draw up a legal agreement. If I would do it and tell him what I wanted, then he would sign it.

I asked the lawyer what I should do. He said I should notify the pension people of our divorce. I was entitled to part of Ben's pension for my retirement. I rang Ben, but he would only discuss it through a lawyer. The pension office explained that, since I had been in Canada, I had worked every year but one. They would have to transfer just $19 from his pension to cover me for that year. I informed the lawyer of what I had been told, as Ben was not having any more discussions. In a divorce situation, the husband usually asks for his wife to be paid out or to pay it when he reached sixty-five. Most prefer to pay it out, and it's settled.

Ben suggested if there was anything I wanted from the house, to put that in also. His brother Frank had sent me a ring with a gold sovereign in it, so I asked if I could have that and a small picture I was fond of. My next request was to ask if he could return half the money for the holidays we'd had together. I didn't look at what I had spent on decorating the house — buying the dishwasher and all the shrubs and curtains — because he had told me at the time that I would have to pay for it. I thought I was asking a very fair amount in this agreement.

When Ben received it, all hell broke loose. He said it was going to be torn up. He agreed I was entitled to some of his pension, but it wouldn't be paid till he was sixty-five. The ring and the picture were fine. Paying for half of the trips he definitely wasn't going to do.

I had given up my nursing with only three months to finish rather than ask him for a penny. I had spent my life looking after him, our home and family, following all his dreams — certainly not my own. It seemed he didn't want me to have anything; it was always all his. He tore up the documents, though they had cost me $300. If I had any more to say, it had to be through the lawyer. As I was about to find out, it was $100 a letter.

Ben's lawyer sent a letter to my lawyer stating that I had no reason to receive any financial support, as I had a good job. I wasn't entitled to his pension. It had been my choice to spend my half on the house, on vacations or anything. He needed only to give me $1,000 as a final settlement.

If he had been in the room when I read that letter, I'm afraid I would have really lost my temper. I just wanted to scream. I never once bought anything for myself out of my half. Most of it had gone back to his house and vacations. If I had gone to England on my own as I'd wanted, it would have been my first use of my half of the money. He had suggested all three trips and had promised to share. So he had lied to his lawyer. I didn't think he could ever hurt me as he had now.

I did everything he asked. He asked me to write a letter stating that I had committed adultery, though the very day I had told him, he'd forgiven me and hadn't wanted me to leave him. What about his adultery? Didn't that count? I said he could keep the ring and the picture. As for the $1,000 as a final offer, he could stuff it. I was going to manage somehow.

I began to think he resented having to give me anything. Maybe he had planned all those holidays and everything else. Was it his way of getting my half of the house money back? Obviously he didn't think any of it was mine, and he knew I wouldn't really say no to him. I ended up replying to seven letters, another $700 down the drain. I just couldn't do this anymore. Any final ones had to wait till the divorce and the lawyers' fees were done. I didn't care if I never saw him again. I was hurt and depressed.

I was on the night shift one night when I turned into a corridor and saw a shadow in a doorway. At first I thought a patient was out of bed, but they were all bedridden and it was all some could do to sit up. When I reached the doorway, the shadow was still there. It seemed as if I was looking at a negative of a photograph, the outline of a lady. I told her I was here. From the shape of the body and the style of hair, I knew immediately it was my grandma. Her face was very sad, and then she was gone. I checked the room and the patients, but all four of them were fast asleep. I hadn't imagined it.

The psychics often say, "If a spirit ever visits you, never be afraid. It is to let you know they love you and want to protect you." I went to the church where my psychic friend worked. She stopped me, asked me to come to her office and told me of a white springer spaniel with brown patches. "He's just going wild here, jumping up and down around you. He's so excited to see you." The tears rolled down my face. I couldn't believe what she had just said. This was our little Scamp, whose leg they had been going to amputate. Next, she said my grandma had been around me all the time lately. Grandma knew I was going through a very rough patch, and she was trying to keep me from hitting rock bottom. "Unfortunately," the psychic said, "you've already hit it. You're in a depression." Her advice was to make a clean break, once and for all. I had tried to do it once before, but I was like a pony still tied to the post.

• • •

One day Ben asked me to meet him. He had a small package with him, a gift. He said he wanted me to have it because I hadn't pushed him for the money. After all we had gone through, here he was actually admitting there was money he owed me. Was he feeling guilty now? I opened the package to find a gold necklace and matching earrings with tiny pearl drops. I thanked him and asked if he wanted to go to the court with me for the divorce. He said he would leave it to the lawyer. We shook hands and said goodbye. I was still in shock after he had gone. He gave me the bill for the jewellery store in case anything went wrong. It was the most expensive jewellery he had ever bought me.

We had been married for twenty-nine years and courted for two and a half years before that. I had given him, in all, thirty-two years of my life. Most of them were very happy. For that, I think I really earned $19 at least.

A Whole New Life

John and I went back to our coffees and our cheap suppers. I couldn't have wished for a better friend. We completely understood what the other had been going through. He went to settle his divorce with his lawyer, only to find his wife's lawyer had delayed it once more. There had been no witness, and his wife told them she had signed under duress. So it started all over again.

One night I got a phone call asking if we could meet right away. I arrived at the café to find him looking as white as a ghost. The RCMP had visited him and asked if he would take his wife in. The chap she had been living with had died suddenly and his children had thrown her out into the street. They asked him to go to the house with them to pick up all her belongings. She suggested he let her live with him, saying she wouldn't mind at all if he still went out with me.

I said I would keep away till it was all sorted out. If he wanted to change his mind and take his wife back, it was his decision. I told him just to let me know. He said he would be in touch soon, and it would be sorted out once and for all. He called me two days later to say she was going to stay with a friend. He looked worn out when I saw him.

Finally his divorce came through, and he said he would like to move nearer to me. He found a vacancy in the apartment at the top of my street. Andrew and the girls really liked him, and I was so glad. We lived in our own places, but he was always there for me. I loved having him around, and I could always be myself with him.

When John asked me to marry him, I had intended never to get married again. But then my divorce went through and I was finally free, and I thought about remarrying non-stop. I realized I didn't want to be without John ever again. I wanted to marry the best friend I'd ever had.

John had come to Canada the same year we had, 1967, but he had lived on the opposite side of the country, in Ontario. Ten years later he came to BC to visit friends, and while he was here he was offered a job. I think fate takes a hand in your life more often than you realize. If he hadn't taken that job, we would never have met.

I thought June would be lovely for the wedding, but it was so near. The girls seemed to be fine about it and wanted to help, but we hadn't heard from Andrew for quite a while and had no idea where he was. I rang his company in Calgary and asked if they could contact him for me, but he had changed companies. They said if they could find anyone who knew where he had gone, they would pass my message on. We set the date for June 15. I called Ben to let him know, and he wished us well.

Everything fell into place. The tiny church in Burnaby held fifty at the most, perfect for the number we had invited. When I came to light the candles in the ceremony, my hands began to shake and my knees to knock. Glancing at Margaret, I saw her knees were the same. I guess it was nerves. The wedding went off without a hitch. My only regret was not having Andrew there to walk me down the aisle. A few days after the wedding he did show up, very sad. He had wanted to be there, and we were all in tears. He promised he would let us know where he was in the future.

After the ceremony we went to a small restaurant, then spent the evening in an Irish pub dancing the night away. At two o'clock we were put in a taxi by the girls, who had arranged everything for the next day. We were taken to a lovely suite in a great downtown hotel, where two glasses and a bottle of champagne awaited us. I didn't usually drink much, but I thought we had to celebrate. I had a tendency to drink quickly, as if it were pop, and in minutes it was gone. I didn't find it at all strong. John poured us the second glass, and then went into the bathroom. When he came out, I must have finished the rest, because I was flat out. I woke up with a hangover, something I'd never had before. My head was bursting.

After lunch we went to the park. As we entered, I saw the grass and wanted to lie down in the lovely sunshine. I quickly sat down and stretched out. Poor John! I slept for three solid hours. When I opened my eyes, he hadn't moved an inch. I felt so bad because we were still right on the edge of the parking lot. I swore this would be my first and last hangover. After the wedding, we moved out of our apartments and into a three-bedroom townhouse in Surrey, where we settled in nicely.

The moment I met John, he jokingly said, "I don't think you're a Pat. You seem more like a Tricia." Only once had I been called that, when I was a student nurse in England. My friend Margaret's little sister was called Tricia, and often Margaret had called me the same. I really liked it. I was starting a new life, so why not a new name?

For my birthday, John bought me my own car plates: TRISH 1. I have to say, I have been his number one ever since. It took my friends a bit longer. The only time it changes is when we visit England, where I still get Pat or Patsy. The family will never see me as anyone else, but I don't mind at all.

Margaret had already returned to school and finished her education, and now she was starting from scratch financially. John suggested we could help by putting a roof over her head at least, so Margaret came to live with us while she worked towards her career goals. Ben decided to marry a Spanish lady he had been seeing for some time, and when Andrew came home for the wedding, he stayed with us. We sent a card to wish the couple well.

Next Ann decided to get married. My sister Barbara rang to say they were all coming, and asked if the girls could be bridesmaids. She said she would get the dresses in England, as she was used to dressing the girls for ballet and pantomimes. Margaret and I had such fun helping select Ann's wedding dress. The groom, M, had a big family, and his mum arranged a dinner for everyone after the rehearsal.

I was worried when Ben and his wife didn't come to the rehearsal. John stood in for Ben, and we were told they wouldn't be at the dinner afterwards, as they had other commitments. Ann was sure he was coming to give her away. I was prepared for anything to happen. I had this terrible feeling they wouldn't come only because we were there.

At the wedding, Ben and his wife were the last to arrive. I automatically went towards them and gave Ben a hug. He almost pushed me over, and his wife brushed past me as I held out my hand to her. Then they walked to the opposite end of the room. They never said a word to John. We quickly got the message: keep away! Afterwards when we sat down to eat, I tried to start a conversation with both of them. Each time, they cut me off, and they didn't speak a word to Babs, David or John.

At home that night, the girls seemed not only tired but sad. Rebecca, Babs's eldest, said they had gone to the wedding in the limousine with their Uncle Ben. They hadn't seen him for a long time, but he didn't even acknowledge them. He didn't speak to them all the night or ask them to dance with him like others did.

Ann and our new son-in-law left on their honeymoon. All I hoped was that they had enjoyed their lovely wedding and had no idea what had happened, though she must have been hurt when they didn't come to her celebrations before the wedding.

● ● ●

Life now was nice and quiet. It was a pleasure to come home from work on my day shifts to find our dinner all ready. I felt so spoiled. John's mum had taught him to cook when he was a young man. I had to remind him I had been cooking for a family for many years, and I didn't think I was likely to change my habits. We made a pact between us — when I cooked he would keep out of the kitchen and vice versa. To this day, he often comes peeping in and I see mischief in his eyes. I still have to chase him out.

Margaret moved out, and we knew we were going to miss her. However, she knew we would both always be there for her. John had never had any children of his own. Since I'd had a hysterectomy, it was too late for me to start again. I'm sure he would have made a very good father. My children could never have wished for a better stepfather. He will always there to help them with anything.

Surviving Disability

I began to notice that whenever I bent down to wind up the beds at work, I had difficulty getting up again. Throughout the years I had worked in extended care units, we were often short staffed and the workloads were heavy. My doctor suggested I wear a steel back brace for support. Oh, it made such a difference — but even with the brace I knew my back was getting worse.

Most of us try to ignore these aches and pains, but sometimes we just can't. At work we used a hoist to lift patients who were unable to get themselves from their beds to their wheelchairs or vice versa. With those who were very heavy, a dead weight, it often took three of us to wind them up from the bed. The hoists were not electrical in those days, so we were damaging all our shoulder joints. On nights, I had trouble pulling the patients over to change them. I had to run around the back and roll them instead, to ease the pain in my shoulders and neck.

Physiotherapy helped at times, but my only real relief was after I had been to my chiropractor. He was always asking me when I was going to slow down. I loved my job too much to let any aches and pains keep me away from it. I never fell behind with my work and always managed to keep up with my younger colleagues. They often commented on how active I was and how good I looked for my age.

John suggested I look into going back to college, as it might give my body a rest. I found a college that was starting a new course to help practical nurses finish the final year. I would still be able to keep my job; the hospital supported anyone who wanted to finish their RN or degree. All I had to do was arrange my medical test and I would be all set for school. My dream was finally about to come true and I would finish what

I had begun so many years ago. My doctor checked my recent problems and had me X-rayed — she was very thorough.

A few days later I received a call to her office. I was totally unprepared for what followed. My doctor walked into the room shaking her head. I had osteoporosis in my upper back and osteoarthritis through the rest of my spine and in both shoulder joints. My lower back was bad, but the upper was severe. Where I'd had my hiatus hernia stapled, there was now a hole in my diaphragm. I had to go on a six-month wait list for surgery and was advised to give up my job immediately.

This couldn't be happening! As usual I thought, I'll get through this. I'll get my chiropractor to fix me. I couldn't give up my job. It was three weeks to Christmas, a time when we needed my money the most. I was almost fifty-one, much too young to give up work. All my life I had been very energetic and hardworking, and I didn't intend to give up easily.

My doctor advised me to speak with my chiropractor, my administrator at the hospital, and the college. I went home in a daze and told John, crying my eyes out. I was off for two days and numb most of the time. My chiropractor told me to take my doctor's advice. If I didn't, he said, I would end up in a wheelchair. The hospital administrator pointed out that I had to think of my own safety as well as the patients'. What would be the consequences if I were injured? If I dropped anybody, I would never forgive myself. The thing that hurt the most was hearing I would probably have to give up my place in the RN course.

I went to my ward to say goodbye. The staff and patients were surprised to hear I was leaving. Our team and patients were my family. I left in a daze, with tears trickling down my face. As I walked away, I prayed fate had something better in store for me. All I felt was total devastation. I had wanted to be a nurse all my life, and this was finally the end to all my hopes and dreams. Everything I loved was being taken away.

Remy and Wendy, my dear friends from work, asked me to come to dinner. When I walked through the door, I found twenty-five people waiting for me. One girl I had worked with on the night shift had just married a nice guy from the hospital and they were supposed to have left on their honeymoon, but they put it off so they could come to this dinner. They made me feel very special.

I had ten weeks of UIC (unemployment insurance) benefits to look forward to, and then things would be very difficult financially. I had to wait six weeks to get it, and in the meantime I had to pay almost $100 a month to keep my disability insurance intact. I was on a six-month wait list for my operation, which required a plastic surgeon. The medical plan did not cover this, and already my medication expenses were adding up. I worried how we were going to be able to pay for it. One wage could only absorb so much. Life became hectic and stressful, as I had to run around filling in paperwork and going to different doctors for tests.

I went to the government office to fill out UIC applications. When you have a steady job, you also have independence. Once you have to rely on someone else for money, you feel as if you are begging for handouts. It doesn't matter that you have already paid into the system or have never taken anything from it. As things get worse, it's very easy to become bitter. There is a tendency to think you're irreplaceable, but you're not. You feel as if no one seems to care, especially your employer.

Seven months passed and I heard nothing from the hospital. I rang the personnel office and spoke to the person in charge, who I had known for years. She suggested I ring the board myself and speak to the people who made the decisions. They told me I would be hearing from them shortly. A week later a letter arrived stating that I had been turned down for a pension. It said back problems were wear and tear at my age, and therefore I could return to my job.

Frustration and anger welled up inside me. My operation had been done, and we were in debt. Did these people understand that I was not just taking a rest? My job, income and future had been taken away from me. I had worked hard all my life and had hoped to continue till retirement.

My doctor was extremely angry. For me to go back to work, they needed her clearance, which she refused to give. The first thing she noticed was that the letter only mentioned my back problem and nothing else. She listed all my other problems, which had been checked out by other doctors too. I had her letter copied, one for the hospital and another one for the union. I told the hospital I would come back only if my doctor agreed, but if I or the patients were hurt in any way, they would have to take full responsibility.

My reflux was getting much worse and I was losing my voice. My vocal cords were scarred, and I was advised to have speech therapy. I could go on the hospital list, but the waiting time was two years and I would have to pay for it. I couldn't afford it. I had no income. John was paying for everything, as my UIC had finished, and it was quite a struggle.

I decided to ring the board and ask when my appeal would be settled. Oh, said the woman I spoke to, they had my appeal, but the delay was due to waiting for my doctor's letter. I asked if she had the appeal form there. She said it was on her desk. I told her the two-page letter from my doctor was stapled to it. "Oh dear," she said, "it is here. We must have missed it somehow. So sorry." I mentioned that our union would be contacting them.

I was at the stage now where if I sat down too long my husband had to pull me up. If I went up the stairs, he literally had to push me up each one. With pernicious anemia and chronic diarrhea, I was totally worn out and extremely stressed. Call it depression and anxiety, along with a total loss of self-esteem. I felt totally useless, a good-for-nothing, and I was pining for the job I had always loved.

Having grown up with responsibilities and some traumas in my life, I expected I could survive anything. No sooner had I told myself this than I was being tested for heart problems. My ECGs were wonky and I had severe chest pain. They thought I might have ischemia, lack of oxygen to the heart muscles, which causes angina. I had no history of heart problems. The eventual conclusion was that it was caused by severe stress. I really felt that I had hit bottom, once again.

Nine months and two weeks had gone by when a cheque arrived with a notification that I finally had my disability pension. I cried with relief, which turned into panic once I read the attached note and forms. They required my doctor to fill in the yearly forms again. After two years, I would be assessed by an RN in my home and maybe by other doctors, and the pension might then cease. I really couldn't face going through all this again. I had to see a counsellor to try to re-train somehow. After a long interview, I was taken aback by what the counsellor said: I was to go home and take my doctor's advice until my health had improved.

John and I moved into a rancher, so there were no more stairs to climb, and I always had my hobbies. I did jigsaws, though I had to stand up and use the countertop, and often watched TV at the same time. I knitted small toys and tea cozies for an annual craft fair, since large items were bad for my arthritic fingers. I made sure to wear my hand supports or elbow brace so as not to damage myself. It wasn't always the knitting that was painful but the sewing afterwards, putting them together. I will never give up my knitting, no matter how bad my fingers are, so I began to go to arthritis exercises at the pool.

I kept looking out for courses I might like to do, but most of them involved a lot of sitting, which wasn't good for my spine. Typing wasn't good for my neck and shoulders. I saw an advert in the paper saying "a lady forced into retirement wishes to meet people in the same situation." I gave her a call and was asked to meet at a local café. Twelve people showed up, all with similar problems. We decided to form a support group, meeting once a month to discuss our concerns.

One of the biggest problems was looking good on the outside. One chap around fifty had been sick and had a withered arm. His doctor encouraged him to mix more because he suffered from depression. He plucked up the courage to go to a local dance, where he bumped into a neighbour, who wondered why he was there while on disability. Others had also been intimidated and made to feel guilty because their disabilities were hidden.

Nobody seems to accept the fact that even if you look good, you can still be in great pain. Most of the time you keep it to yourself and say "I'm fine" only because nobody wants to hear about your aches and pains and the troubles you have getting by on limited funds. We pay the same taxes as everyone else out there. Would these people prefer to see us all in wheelchairs?

There are also people who resent the fact that you are at home getting paid and they still have to get up and go to work. They don't think about what you had to give up, or that maybe you'll never be able to return to work. Larry Wark of the Canadian Auto Workers Union said, "No one can replace the dignity of having a job to go to every day." I couldn't agree more. To the people who do begrudge us our disability pensions, we would be very happy to take over your jobs anytime. You are also very welcome to come and take over our illnesses.

This support group helped me survive my own crisis. I would encourage anyone with any kind of disability or illness to take any support offered. It does really help. It certainly helped to reduce the stress.

Sadness and depression bring life to a halt. You can drag yourself through each day for a long time. One day you have to face the fact that you may be on this earth for a very long time. Do you want to live in this miserable state for the rest of your life? Or are you going to make an effort to try to do something more worthwhile?

You may see your family or friends trying to cope with their lives too. It may be illness, relationships, alcoholism, bankruptcy, drugs, business problems, divorce, death or abuse (sexual or otherwise). You name it, and you will find someone out there has gone through it. There are times when you feel helpless and angry that you cannot solve it for them. What can you do? Just let them know you're there for them no matter what.

Every Christmas I went back to visit my old friends at the hospital. At times it was an effort to go, because every time I came home, I started weeping. Disability is kind of like death — you mourn for everything and everyone you have lost. After ten years of visits, I found only five people left that I had known. A lot of the staff I had known were on disability or had passed away.

For the first time I came home and did not weep. Somehow I felt at peace. I actually felt I had achieved some kind of balance in my life and had accepted my fate. I knew I had survived my disability. I believe that if you can survive disability, you can survive anything in life.

Regarding disability

In the Guardian I recently read
Their cameras would be out, it said.
They have learned a lot of truth, they think.
So their information made me think.

Many a time, many a day,
An old acquaintance came my way.
The common phrase you're bound to hear
Is "Well, you look much better than me, my dear.
What have you been doing? You look so good?"

My heart it flutters, I'm in fear,
for I've been on disability for the last ten year.
I feel shame, but I'm not a bum,
who doesn't want to work, old chum?
No one knows the pain inside
That's always something we try to hide.
For our friends would really start to moan
If we were always out to groan.
I lost my job and income too,
Also the plans I made for my lifetime too.
My husband, who's my bright shining star,
Helped me to try and keep my car,
For there's no buses and a mile's too far.
Without my husband I have to declare,
My life would be dead, and I'd be on welfare.

There are days I can't go out because of the fear
That I know that I have chronic diarrhea.
Depending just how long it lasts,
My routine and my plans just go like a blast.
The garden's appealing, the sun and the air,
But can I really go out there? Do I really dare?
For I have a severe reflux, and each time I bend,
The bile's running out of the other end.
Well, folks, perhaps now you will see
That the sickness is on the inside of me.
Osteoporosis, pernicious anemia, arthritis and such.
A back brace. As on both hands. Oh! It's really a bust.

On happiness, well, I really would shout
If my sickness one day could really jump out.
For I'd have a new life, a job, and you'd see
That my heart and my face would be filled full of glee.
You have to go through it, and I'll hope and will say
That I hope it will never come your way!
For disability is the worst thing that I have ever done,
And I'd never wish it on anyone.

This poem was printed in our union newspaper.

Moving On

As my health improved, I asked myself what I could do for those who needed help. What had bothered me the most in extended care was that we hadn't been able to spend enough time with people when they were dying. I remembered one particular time, when a lady who had been with us a long time was sick. On evening shifts, when we had finished washing a patient, one of us would run to see if she was okay and give her a hug. It would have been nice if we could have sat for a while and held her hand. One night when Remy and I were working, our lady was alive one minute, and five minutes later she had passed away. We had the job of laying her out. Our hearts were so full, but we couldn't say a word. We both took her to the morgue and as we said goodbye to her and the doors closed behind us, we looked at one another and sobbed our hearts out.

Dealing with grief is not for everyone. There are many other groups out there who need your help. It can be very rewarding to concentrate on someone else. You tend to forget your own problems. You find yourself coping better and seem to have more self-worth. I decided the best plan for me was to volunteer with the hospice. In addition, I went to monthly arthritis meetings and became a volunteer at health fairs.

The hospice course took a number of weeks. I learned about the different stages of grief and anger that most of us go through and how we can help people cope with them. We went to a palliative care ward in the hospital, then we began sitting with the patients on a regular basis.

I went to sit with the chemotherapy patients in the clinic. We would welcome the patients with a cup of tea or something they liked, stand by while the nurse hooked them up to their medication, and then sit beside them. Over time, we got to know the patients well. Often new patients were nervous. As in nursing, you recognize the people who want to talk and those who don't. You must listen to what they are saying and give them the opportunity to speak. It can often take a while before they open up and get things off their chests.

The hospice encouraged us to keep a diary of our own reactions and feelings, and then we discussed any problems at the meetings. It was something had I tended to do all my life, for if you have nobody to tell your troubles to, it helps to get your thoughts down on paper. After the training we were expected to do a minimum of twelve hours a month and attend the meetings once a month.

I spent a whole day in the clinic and a day in the Palliative Care Ward. Then I was asked to visit people in their homes, which was much different than the hospital. Patients needed to sleep a lot. They might talk for fifteen minutes or so, then go to sleep. Most times the family asked you to stay with them and have a cup of tea. Often it was the family who really needed your company. The stress of looking after parents or loved ones was very hard on them.

I was asked to visit a patient named Pearl on the Surgical Ward. A week before, she'd had a second amputation on her leg. I had dealt with missing limbs and eyes as a nurse — glass eyes had to be taken out and cleaned before being put back, and we'd also had patients with legs missing and one with an artificial leg that we had to put on daily. When I walked into Pearl's room I held my breath, trying to be ready for anything. But there she was, sitting up and smiling.

She was expecting me, and she was very welcoming. She said she was doing well and readily explained that both legs had been removed years ago, one to the groin and the other to the knee. The one at the knee now had to be taken off at the groin also. She seemed to be well adjusted to her wheelchair. I visited her for seven weeks and then she was transferred to a private home in south Surrey. A week or two later, they asked me if I would visit her again.

Over the years we became very good friends. She was always involved in the home's activities and invited me to join in many with her. John often made her special cookies, which she loved. Our niece Rebecca was visiting from England once and Pearl asked me if I would bring Rebecca to see her. We took her to the park on a beautiful sunny day. Over the years there were times when Pearl was really ill, but she always came through.

One day after giving me a picture of herself when she was young, she told me her brother might take her home with him to Kelowna for a visit. We were going on holiday for two weeks, so I popped in to see her the day before we left. She wished me a lovely holiday and said, "If I'm not here when you get back, just remember that I will always love you." I thought she might be going to her family, but I had a very strange feeling. It crossed my mind that maybe she was saying goodbye to me for good.

The day after we got back, I rang the home. Quite often she sat near the desk and they would hand her the phone, so I asked if Pearl was around. There was a silence, but I heard some breathing. The receptionist asked who I was. I told her I was the hospice lady, and she said all she could reveal was that Pearl had passed away three days ago. She had been cremated and her family had picked up her ashes this morning. They were taking them to Sicamous to be scattered. I would never forget her.

Three weeks before Christmas, the hospice put up a lovely tree of remembrance in the lobby. Volunteers received donations and placed cards on the tree in honour of those who had passed away. I was sitting there when I received a phone call from Remy to tell me a colleague of ours had died.

Four of us were to go to the funeral — Remy, Lily, Wendy and I. When I arrived to pick everyone up from Remy's, I was told that Lily, who had recently been in a car accident, had just had a bad reaction to a drug and had gone into such severe shock that she'd had to be placed on life support.

We arrived at the funeral just as everyone there was finding out the sad news: Lily's husband had asked to take her off life support. How we made it through I will never know. The pretty happy girl from the Philippines (like Remy), just fifty years old and with a husband and teenage daughter, was not there anymore.

At this point I knew I couldn't take any more grief. After eight years in the hospice I realized it was time to go. I had loved what I was doing, but also you have to recognize when you are burnt out.

• • •

With three children, I was hoping someday to see some grandchildren. While I was waiting for this to happen, I decided to do what I had done before I married — fill our bottom drawer, as we called it then. I would fill it with things for babies. I bought tiny baby toys and blankets, even a tiny hippopotamus for potty training. Wearing my hand supports, I became very busy knitting. I lost count of all the jackets, hats and booties I made.

Ann and M had been married for seven years. As much as they wanted children, it had never happened and there seemed little chance it ever would. One week Ann and M asked us over to Sunday lunch. It had been a while — they had their own business and seemed to work non-stop. When we sat down to lunch, both John and I began to think there was something wrong. M seemed very fidgety or jittery. We had never seen him like that before. Suddenly he stood up and said, "Ann, I just can't sit and eat. I can't do this. You must tell them now." Ann looked at M and started smiling. "We have to tell you that we're expecting a baby," she said. I almost fell off the edge of the chair. It was a miracle.

We finally became proud grandparents. They had a lovely daughter, and she was certainly in a hurry to get here, arriving a full month early. Such a tiny baby, slightly over five pounds. Her name was Amanda Grace. We met Ben at the hospital and he was as excited as we were.

• • •

When Amanda was three, Margaret decided to get married to a wonderful fellow, R. The groom's family came in from Winnipeg, Andrew came home from up North, and Uncle Frank came from England, as did John's sister and her husband.

Ann and M decided to do a family buffet in their garden, as the weather was great. I walked into the garden to see Frank talking to Ben's wife. As soon as Frank saw me, he jumped up shouting and gave me a big hug. I knew right away that nothing had changed between us. He was talking with us when Ben came out of the house. Ben smiled and shook hands with me across the table. Then he offered his hand to John. I was really happy, because we would be spending the next few days all together.

The wedding went off very well. We all enjoyed it, and then we danced the night away. Frank spent some time at our house and at Ann's. Andrew had to leave after Margaret and R went on their honeymoon. A week later, we went on a cruise to Alaska with John's sister and her husband. The cruise was wonderful. In fact, the whole year was the best of many.

A Shock From the Past

After Margaret's wedding I had the urge to start learning again. I decided to take a course in counselling, as I thought it would be a great help in my volunteering. We learned about the theory and practice of counselling, psychoanalytical therapy, group therapy, and cross-cultural counselling. Most of the people in our class had joined for a reason, perhaps alcoholism in the family, drugs or abuse. Having gone through such difficulties, they wanted to help others. It was amazing what some of them had gone through for years, never saying a word. I guess I had done the same, but somehow I had put it in the past. I didn't think I had let it ruin my life once I had got away. But sometimes people have to let it out and do something about it to protect others.

Many read their stories, and our teacher was overwhelmed by what she heard. This class opened up to her more than any had before. I discovered I could discuss it without going into the really intimate details. I knew I could tell John if I needed to, because he had gone through something similar with his ex-wife. It was much easier to discuss these things with somebody who had been through it. I passed with good marks, and hoped I could help other people with all I had learned.

Around the same time I began to get more calls from my sister, many lasting an hour or more. I had a feeling she had been drinking. Once or twice she mentioned a couple of things I had done, and it sounded a bit mean. I came to the conclusion that something in her own life was making her very unhappy. I had to find out what it was, for both our sakes.

One day she called and I had no doubt she'd been drinking. Her voice was a bit slurred and she was a little mean again. She accused me of going to Canada and leaving her behind. I told her I was hurt to think she believed I could do something like that deliberately. I knew there was definitely something very wrong. Then she said, "You were always the quiet one. I was sick of hearing that I should be like you."

"I was sick of telling Mum and Dad not to say that," I told her. "We were almost thirteen years apart." I wanted to pull my hair out. When she was growing up, they hadn't done to her what they'd done to me. Why? Because she was outspoken and she hadn't let them. On her visit to Norwich she told me she stayed out late and went drinking with her friends, and that she'd told Mum and Dad they weren't going to do to her "what they did to our Pat." Someone must have told her how they were with me, because she was only five when I left home, or maybe she had a good memory and actually remembered seeing it herself.

I asked her then whether, if David had wanted to emigrate, she would have gone with him or let him go on his own. There was no reply, so I said, "You would probably have done what I did if you loved him."

Suddenly she said, "But you were the quiet one, and you got away from Dad. If I'd been like you, he might have left me alone. Because I wasn't, he went after me."

Oh God, no! Please, no!

I held my breath and asked her straight out, "Barbara, did Dad sexually abuse you?"

"Yes!" she said, and she began to cry.

We'd both had the same problem and had kept it to ourselves all these years.

"Babs," I said, "what you've just told me happened to me too."

"Oh no! You were the quiet one."

"I thought it was because I was the quiet one that it happened to me. Because Dad could be sure I was too scared to tell anyone."

She was shaken. "I can't believe this," she said.

I said it was true. I tried to explain how he had manipulated me. How he had threatened to go after my friends if I didn't do what he wanted. How in the end, I stopped bringing anyone home and went to their homes instead. Babs had no trouble recognizing that — it had been exactly the same for her.

We were both crying by then, and we needed some sleep after three hours on the phone. I told her I would write straight away. I knew she had been drinking, and I had a feeling that if I didn't put it in writing she might not remember what I'd said, or she might think it was all a dream.

I thought back to what Dad had said to me when he was ill. I had told him to leave it all in the past, that it was best there. Since then, I'd felt it was gone totally, but now it had reared its ugly head once more. Mum always told us never to use the word hate to anyone about anything, but I found it was the first word that entered my head. It seemed to be the word I wanted and, being angry, I really did — I hated him for what he had done to my sister.

When I was fifteen and very close to a nervous breakdown, I thought he was sorry for what had happened. He never touched me or said anything abusive again, and I felt that I had my dad back. When I left home, I never thought of the possibility that it could happen to Babs; it had only happened to me because of my terrible shyness. My goodness, was I naive! My heart sank. She was just under six when I left. I thought he had learned his lesson.

She was nineteen when we came to Canada, and before that we lived in Norwich for four and a half years. If we had never moved, I would still have been in Hull, and then she would have had at least a chance to tell me. I was deeply sorry that I hadn't been there when she needed me most. If I had found out all this in England, shy or not, I would have somehow seen him in jail. From things I have put together since, I see him as a real pedophile.

Looking back, I think after all it was a blessing that our children were away from him. I dread to think of what he might have done to them if they had been around him. I asked Babs if she had told David or her girls. At times she had tried to drop hints, but she hadn't thought anyone would believe her. She had no trust for men and had watched her girls like a hawk in case anyone touched them. It was a blessing that Babs had her children after Dad died. Otherwise, she might have gone out of her mind worrying when he was near them.

I asked Ann if she remembered anything about her granddad, and her reply was "Not really." Her only memory was that he had squeezed her too tightly when her asthma was bad and she'd felt she couldn't breathe very well. Maybe someone up there was protecting all our children after seeing what he did to us.

Babs rang again after receiving my letter. She hadn't remembered what I'd told her, because she'd been drunk, and when she read it she was blown over. Now she knew we had talked about it. No one else had ever known. To this day, she tells me what a shock it was to hear that from me.

I was very worried about her and wrote to Aunty Ivy. Someone near her needed to know what was happening, and there was no one closer. I knew Ivy would be upset, but she would look out for Babs. Babs certainly needed help. It was obvious she had told her own family something but they had never believed it. They probably never would be any help.

I asked her to seek out a group that dealt with that sort of thing. She did find one and it must have helped her, because later on she began to help others. I was so happy she had come this far. I told her I wanted to write all this down. I wanted anyone who had been through something similar to know there is help out there. If it helped only one person, I would be happy. Maybe one day Babs will pick up a pen and do the same thing. I will encourage her as she has encouraged me ever since I mentioned writing it down.

I still can't believe it happened to both of us. I was thirty years old when I came to Canada, and lived here forty-two years before I found out. Babs and I have discussed so much together since. With her encouragement, I knew I had to tell people. There are far too many people out there who have gone through the same things and are still going through them. I strongly advise them to stand up to any abuse and to go for help. Not like us all those years ago. Because we were too scared to tell.

I don't think one of my relatives really knows what kind of life we had, either in England or in Canada, only what Mum told them. I know what I have written may cause a few fireworks, but I hope they realize that I felt I had to write it. Not just for me, but for my sister, and for everyone out there who has faced abuse or domination. Today bullying alone has cost families their children due to suicide. If a family knows about these things happening, please do something about it. Family support is greatly needed. Victims must speak out.

When I mentioned to Ben what Dad had done, he went for a run. He came back saying he never wanted me to leave, but he never mentioned what I'd told him about my dad, not to this day. He really didn't want to know. It seemed I was right in not telling him before. I was very lucky that I was able to put it all in the past. I refused to let it haunt me or ruin the rest of my life. Now everyone will know, and I, with Barbara, will not be afraid. Because this still goes on, and it has to stop.

Anger

Anger comes and anger goes.
It sometimes even comes to blows.
We let off steam, call it frustration.
It's certainly popular around the nation.
We kick, we scream, to get it out.
Anger is what it's all about.

Control is what is really needed,
But most of us, we never heed it.
Anger makes us very glum,
Upsetting almost everyone.
We strike out verbally, or throw out fists.
Then we start to feel like twits.
We know when we are out of control.
We don't know what to do, that's all.

We need some guidance, please pursue.
We have to learn what we can do.
Recognize, with all these factions
There's a reason or cause for all our actions.
With thought and understanding that if we really share
We just might clear our problems and our anger from the air.

Two Different Worlds

I thought I knew what stress was from growing up through the war years, struggling just to put food on the table, wondering if we would survive, and watching people around us lose their loved ones. When we could afford those little extras, we really appreciated what we had. We were so used to going without. The one thing I will always remember is that we were always there for each other. We laughed, chatted and sang our hearts out together.

Today people are under a different kind of stress. They just don't have time to stop and smell the roses, as we used to stay. They can't or they won't. Wherever they go, their computer goes too, and so do their phones. When we finally could afford to have a meal out now and again, a restaurant was a place to relax for a while and enjoy a meal. Nowadays cell phones are ringing everywhere. Movie theatres tell you to turn your phone off, but there is always someone who ignores their request. Children are losing the natural way to socialize.

All these electronics are wonderful, but now they are becoming an obsession. I see adults as well as children walking through crosswalks texting or talking on their phones and not looking either way to see if any traffic is approaching. It seems there has been a great loss of common sense. I wonder what is so urgent on the phone, walking or driving, that you have to risk your lives. I can remember standing near a Belisha beacon (a big yellow ball on a pole at the edge of our crosswalks) and being made to repeat "Eyes right, eyes left, then right again. If all clear, then quick march." It is still in my head whenever we cross the road.

Families may do more sports nowadays, in the way of more expensive hobbies — golf and hockey, for example. Like the cost of a home to live in, it is all becoming too much. Both parents have to go out to work to afford these things, so they have to have their children looked after by someone else. I feel I have lived in two different worlds.

My greatest fear these days is for the homeless. Everyone should have a roof over their heads. When I grew up, most people didn't own their own homes. England had a very good system for houses for the poorest. If you were on the streets, it was usually because you chose to be. Churches helped out and charities like the Salvation Army were there for everyone. I never saw food banks like we have today in BC. Ordinary families and seniors have to choose between rent, food and medication because they don't have enough pension or income. Vancouver is an extremely expensive place to live, and nothing seems to be done about it.

• • •

After my disability, we did well, really. John had a decent job. I thank God that I was born when and where I was. Having learned how not to spend when we couldn't afford it, we could stretch our money a bit more. When we had extra, we enjoyed spending it, but there's no doubt that it's debt that drags you down. We still had a small mortgage, and at seventy-two years old we wished it wasn't there.

Margaret, who lived on Vancouver Island now, suggested we buy property over there, as it was much cheaper than on the Lower Mainland. We went over to the Island and spoke to a realtor, and realized we could pay off our mortgage and have a little bit left over to travel. After lots of thinking, we took a house in Ladysmith, a cute little town known for its beautiful Christmas lights. The house was 2,350 square feet and cost us half what we would have paid on the mainland. John had trained in England as a carpenter and joiner and had always put it to good use, and he decided he would like to renovate the basement.

We put our old home up for sale the day before Canada Day. Going to bed that night, I told John I had a strange feeling that someone was coming the next day to buy it. "Oh, you and those funny feelings," he said. At eight thirty the next morning, the phone rang. It was the realtor's office in a bit of a panic. Could we possibly let someone in to see our home that evening? I still remember the look on John's face. The next morning, another phone call came to say we had an offer. We had moved into our new house within a month, feeling we had done the right thing.

The family came to visit us in our new home. Andrew brought his wife and his boat, and Ann and M came with our granddaughter Amanda.

Ben and his wife stayed with Margaret and her husband. We were able to sit down together and we got along very well. Life seemed too short now to keep getting upset about things. We spent the day having a picnic on the beach and then taking rides in the boat.

Andrew and his partner seemed perfect for each other, like two peas in a pod. They had met out in the bush, where she was the cook for the camp. She'd had a hard life — her first husband had died young, and she'd had two young children to bring up. She went through years of fighting a brain tumour, which was in remission. When she told me she had lived in Fort Nelson, I thought, No wonder she and Andrew seem so alike! She certainly knew the North. They were at home out in the wild, and liked to spend their holidays up in the Yukon, a place Andrew adores tremendously. In their free time, they went out fishing on their boat. That summer, they decided to come to the Island to camp and fish, and Ann's daughter Amanda came with them. Amanda's dad had taken her hiking since she was tiny, so she had a great love for the outdoors. While camping on the Island, they saw whales, seals and bears.

We are about twenty minutes down the highway from Margaret and R's, so we often meet up and go to the movies. I guess we finally feel at home on the Island. Life seems much more relaxed.

• • •

So many things have happened in my life as I look back. I am grateful to have seen so much. What I have written here are my own stories, no one else's. I was hoping to make you all laugh, and I had a giggle or two myself. However, as I was sitting here typing, I realized that I have been drowning my old typewriter in tears. I am not only writing these memories, I am also reliving all these moments again.

I am so lucky to have had so much love in my life, but there has also been much sadness, some of it so sad, I couldn't bring myself to write about it. I want everyone to understand that I never, ever wanted to hurt anyone. If anything in this book hurts anyone in the family, then I ask you for forgiveness. I thank you all for having the patience to read this.

Like many others I ask myself, as I did many years ago, What am I doing here? Are we here to learn lessons to make us better people? Or is this just hell on earth? I really don't like what I see in the world anymore. There are times when no matter how you try to help, you just can't. It's a helplessness I find hard to describe. Is it because we have to help ourselves? Every year when we go to the cenotaph and I watch the old planes up in the sky, my heart is full and tears wash my face. We were celebrating the end of our old world wars, and it's wonderful to see so many young people joining in.

Nothing can ever be perfect, but if we can each do a little, gradually we can make changes. Through it all, I look back and one thing I know — no matter what has happened, I love both my parents. Love and hate can be very wearing. Hate is a waste of time and life is too short. I would love to see a world where everyone is safe and secure, with a roof over their heads and plenty to eat. As I say this, I think of a lovely song, "If I Ruled the World," sung by Sir Harry Secombe. It describes a world full of freedom, love and peace, a world we all desire.

When I reached the age of about sixty-eight, I finally found a balance. It is very hard to describe, because I am not really sure how or when it happened. I only know that now I have a feeling of contentment within and I handle things much better, or more easily. It is an acceptance that there will always be some problems — if not my own, then those of family or friends. During the horrible points in my early life I would ask myself, When is this going to end? I wondered what would happen to me next. Yet now I am sure in my heart that no matter what comes my way, I will be able to deal with it. I feel the real outcome of this is that I do not worry as much as I did in the past. I have to get on with it no matter what. Whether it comes from experience or age, I may never know. I take one day at a time and just do the best I can. Looking back on my life, I can say it has been busy and interesting. There has been lots of love and much heartbreak, in spite of which I look forward to many more years.

As I approach eighty, I intend to go on fighting no matter what happens in my life. Whatever has happened in the past, I eventually got through it. I am still here and I have survived. My husband and family will always be the loves of my life.

My book has finally ended. My sister Barbara will be pleased our stories are finally out. We can stand together and face everyone.

Now neither of us is scared to tell.

Taking time

The stars in the heavens look down and see
All the beauty surrounding both you and me.
The mountains, the rivers the land and the sea
Will stay and will reign through eternity.

You and I have our lives but for a short while,
Yet we barely take time to stop and to smile.
Our lives are so busy, we're all in a rush.
When we realize life's over, there's a long quiet hush.
When we stand by the graveside, then all of us see
How precious each life on this this planet should be.

To take time to admire everything that's around
From the songs of the birds to the ants on the ground.
To relax, breathe fresh air, with a sky oh so blue!
A sun shining bright that will warm us all through.

Take a moment to think, even say a small prayer
Tell your loved one and friends that you really do care.

Look up to the stars on a beautiful night,
When the full moon is bathed in its silvery light.
When you stop for a moment, you'll realize with awe
All the beautiful things that God left at your door.

Life's full of good things, but we often forget.
So live life and enjoy. Have no time for regret.
Do your best every day. Who could ask you for more?
Then to the greatest of heights your spirit will soar.

I sit and ponder where I have been

In my middle age, as 1 l look back, 1 see the world and 1 wonder
Where we have been and to where we have come,
    and I'd like to vent my anger.
Once rivers flowed so very clean and nature we all cherished.
Today, ravished in waste and oil, the fish and the wildlife perish.
Our food we spray with pesticide and it's in the air we breathe.
Our oxygen diminishes as we cut down all our trees.

A world that's full of anarchy, we are killing off each other.
How can we do this to those we've loved, destroy our own dear brother?
A world of hate and racism, of drugs and Aids that we have spread.
Starving people everywhere, they may as well be dead.
For they don't have a chance at a decent life,
    or dreams and hopes they have cherished.
Ethnic cleansing brought them down, and so thousands may have perished.

As 1 look back on the world 1 have loved
    and the things 1 held most dear,
Our politics and our moral state are the things 1 have come to fear.

Reflections

On Trish's thoughts on disability, depression, volunteering, burnout, health-care and counselling:

The stress of knowing your hopes, dreams and plans for the future have gone for good plus coping with a painful illness, unable to do regular things, leads to depression. It particularly hurts when people say you look so good. That's on the outside; hidden inside, everything feels damaged. Coping with the loss of income and waiting nine months for a pension, was extremely hard on my family and me.

My volunteering work was really important to me. Even though I had loved nursing, when people passed away I always regretted that we hadn't been able to spend more time with them. Once I felt better, I had a choice: I could sit and cry; or I could think of others, helping them and thereby feeling better myself. I joined the Surrey Hospice Society near where I lived. I took a course and volunteered on a palliative care ward, working in the chemo treatment section. I also went out to homes to talk with patients and their families. Then I began a two-year course to become a counsellor. After coping with my illness for years, I was on the mend; and feeling better, and I somehow found a balance in my life.

One thing we were taught, however, was that a person in our line of work could burn out, and we must recognize it when it happens. It happened to me eight years later, when between my family and my husband's we lost ten relatives in six months. Then two of my closest nursing friends suddenly passed; one was on life support in the same hospital where I did my volunteering. I knew I was burnt out and had to have a break.

Three months later; I became interested in arthritis, as it was one of the conditions I had myself. First I went to meetings, and then I got involved in setting up public health fairs, where people could discuss their problems. I enjoyed meeting people and helping them. There was no payment for my counselling or time. I did this for twenty-two years, and it was worth it — time well spent.

Since we moved to Vancouver Island, I have concentrated on writing my book. I've recently come out of a long serious illness. I made it again, and I will keep on fighting. There is always someone out there worse off than I am. If I can help one person in this life, I will be happy.

Tricia Cook was born in Hull, Yorkshire, before World War II, studied nursing, married, and immigrated to Canada with her husband and three children.

Writing poetry helped her survive the rigours of life in northern British Columbia, before she moved to Metro Vancouver. There she worked, got further healthcare training, divorced and eventually remarried. Forced to retire because of a disability, she went on to take courses and to volunteer in hospice and arthritis care for thirty years, often acting as a counsellor. When she found out her younger sister had also been abused, she knew she had to tell others to speak up.

After moving to Vancouver Island, she started typing this revealing memoir.

www.ingramcontent.com/pod-product-compliance
Lightning Source LLC
Chambersburg PA
CBHW072139090426
42739CB00013B/3227